Luscious

Tender

Juicy

Luscious

RECIPES FOR PERFECT

Tender

TEXTURE IN DINNERS,

Juicy

DESSERTS, AND MORE

Kathy Hunt

The Countryman Press
A Division of W. W. Norton & Company
Independent Publishers Since 1923

Copyright © 2021 by Kathy Hunt

All photography by the author except for the following pages:
Page 9: © haoliang/iStockphoto.com; 19: © StephanieFrey/iStockphoto.com; 24: © Sean Dippold/
iStockphoto.com; 51: © ClarkandCompany/iStockphoto.com; 57: © bhofack2/iStockphoto
.com; 58: © Tatiana Volgutova/iStockphoto.com; 65: © LauriPatterson/iStockphoto.com;
116: © EzumeImages/iStockphoto.com; 119: © Ale02/iStockphoto.com; 128: © Lara Hata/
iStockphoto.com; 152: © Adam Sargent/iStockphoto.com; 158: © AlexPro9500/iStockphoto
.com; 184: © LuluDurand/iStockphoto.com; 187: © sara_winter/iStockphoto.com; 193:
© bhofack2/iStockphoto.com

For information about permission to reproduce selections from this book, write to
Permissions, The Countryman Press, 500 Fifth Avenue, New York, NY 10110

For information about special discounts for bulk purchases, please contact
W. W. Norton Special Sales at specialsales@wwnorton.com or 800-233-4830

Manufacturing through Imago
Book design by Allison Chi
Production manager: Devon Zahn

Library of Congress Cataloging-in-Publication Data

Names: Hunt, Kathy, author.
Title: Luscious, tender, juicy : recipes for perfect texture in dinners, desserts, and more /
    Kathy Hunt.
Description: New York, NY : The Countryman Press, a division of W. W. Norton & Company
    Independent Publishers Since 1923, [2021] | Includes bibliographical references and index.
Identifiers: LCCN 2021024857 | ISBN 9781682686614 | ISBN 9781682686621 (epub) Subjects:
    LCSH: Cooking. | LCGFT: Cookbooks.
Classification: LCC TX714 .H856 2021 | DDC 641.5–dc23
LC record available at https://lccn.loc.gov/2021024857

The Countryman Press
www.countrymanpress.com

A division of W. W. Norton & Company, Inc.
500 Fifth Avenue, New York, NY 10110
www.wwnorton.com

10 9 8 7 6 5 4 3 2 1

For Drena, Shanae, Faye, and Imani,
who inspired this cookbook,
and
for Sean

Contents

Introduction

MY MOTIVATION FOR WRITING A COOK-book on luscious, tender, and juicy foods boils down to one dreaded word: *moist*. Utter the word *moist* to some people and they giggle. Mention it at a party and friends will groan. Accidentally bring it up in conversation with acquaintances and listen as the conversation grinds to an embarrassed halt. It has become one of the most despised words of this century. Yet, that wasn't always the case.

During the 14th century, when this adjective first entered the English lexicon, it held no negative connotations. It simply meant that something contained moisture. From the 14th through the 20th century, cooks used it to describe everything from baked breads and cakes to roasted meats and vegetables. If a food had a soft, lush consistency, it was called moist.

Today, though, it makes most people, including my family and friends, cringe. In 2014, researchers at Ohio's Oberlin College and Texas's Trinity University set out to determine why *moist* had transformed from a handy descriptor to a loathed term. They came up with three theories. The first deals with the vowel-consonant sounds of the word itself and how that sound provokes a negative reaction; some respondents in the study compared hearing the sound *oyst* to hearing nails dragged over a chalkboard. The second theory suggests that the facial muscles used to say "moist" are the same facial muscles used to express disgust. The third involves bodily functions and how "moist" reminds people of them.

Why, or how, moist has turned into a taboo word is not my main concern. Bringing it back to where it belongs, as an accurate description of luscious, tender, and/or juicy food? That is my mission and the goal of this cookbook.

Rather than feel horrified, I believe that we should embrace the term. Some of our best culinary creations stem from this very trait. Think about banana bread, hummus, mashed potatoes, quiche, meatloaf, and carrot cake. You can't describe the feel of these dishes as wet. You can't call them damp, as in, "Yum, that's a damp piece of cake." You certainly wouldn't say "Wow! This hummus is the opposite of dry." That would be silly. I bet that you can't refer to these foods as ambrosial and keep a straight face. There is no getting around it. One of the reasons people love these foods are because they are moist.

What gives food a moist, luscious texture? To state the obvious, it contains moisture. Some vegetables and fruits, including cucumbers, mushrooms, potatoes, strawberries, and tomatoes, possess a large amount of liquid. In fact, tomatoes and cucumbers consist of roughly 95 percent water and 5 percent solids. Mushrooms and strawberries contain a bit less, about 92 percent water, while potatoes have 80 percent. Put any of these ingredients in a recipe and you increase the amount of moisture in the resulting dish.

The presence of fat also produces this toothsome texture. Some fats, such as butter, contain water. As I already pointed out, water increases moisture content. Other fats, such as olive or vegetable oil, are liquids and, by nature, moist. They add to the silky texture of baked goods, spreads, and fried foods.

In addition to ingredients, how long you cook a dish influences its texture. If you bake, roast, grill, or fry anything for too long, it will dry out. If you braise, boil, steam, or poach beyond the recommended time, you won't craft an opulent meal. Instead you will make a soppy, disintegrating mess.

One of the keys to good cooking, and making food moist, is to pay attention. Monitor the food's progress as it cooks. Check its internal temperature. Add more liquids or fats if needed. Cover the food to prevent overbrowning and to increase the moisture in the dish. Uncover it to reduce the risk of sogginess. Follow this simple advice and you can make a marvelously moist repast any time.

Not convinced that we should add *moist* to our vocabulary and incorporate lusciousness in our cooking? Join me on this journey through the world of moist foods. When we reach the final recipe, you can decide whether to banish or embrace this term. I suspect that you will join me in celebrating dishes that are luscious, tender, and juicy—or moist. After all, it is the desired consistency and the perfect description for a wide range of delectable foods.

My Interest in Bringing Moisture Back into the Kitchen

Chances are, if you can't characterize the food on your plate as being as dry as a soda cracker, as crisp as a kale chip, as gooey as a sundae, or as runny as a soup, that food is going to be one thing and one thing only. That food is moist.

As a kid, I rarely had the chance to enjoy luscious homemade meals. My mother, the self-appointed cook of our household, possessed little enthusiasm for the kitchen. As a result, she made our suppers about as succulent and soft as sandpaper. Whether as an act of rebellion or sheer desperation, I started to tinker in the kitchen and look for ways to bring moisture into our desiccated dinners.

Through reading cookbooks, attending cooking school, interviewing and cooking alongside skilled chefs and home cooks, and a lot of trial-and-error, I learned to add moisture through a liquid or fat. Other times I relied on moisture-laden ingredients or moist-heat cooking techniques.

That brings us to the next sections. We'll start with a list of moist ingredients, then we'll consider some cooking techniques.

Moist Ingredients

To create luscious and tender dishes, you will use some inherently moist ingredients. These include such fruits and vegetables as:

Apple	Lettuce (all varieties)
Apricot	Melons (cantaloupe,
Asian pear	casaba, honeydew,
Bean (green)	watermelon)
Beet	Mushroom
Bell pepper	Nectarine
Berries (blackberry,	Okra
blueberry, raspberry,	Onion
strawberry)	Parsley (flat-leaf)
Bok choy	Parsnip
Broccoli	Peach
Brussels sprout	Pineapple
Cabbage (red and green)	Plum
Carrot	Potato
Cauliflower	Pumpkin
Celery	Radish
Citrus (grapefruit,	Rhubarb
lemon, lime, orange)	Rutabaga
Cranberry	Spinach
Cucumber	Squash (butternut,
Eggplant	spaghetti, summer)
Fig	Swiss chard
Greens (beet, collard,	Tomato
dandelion, fiddlehead,	Turnip
kale, mustard, turnip)	Zucchini

Other ingredients lending moisture to our cooking include:

Butter	New York strip, rib
Cheese—soft or fresh	eye, T-bone)
(Brie, Camembert,	Oil (grapeseed, olive,
cottage cheese, cream	peanut, sesame)
cheese, fresh moz-	Oily fish (anchovy,
zarella, mascarpone,	butterfish, herring,
quark, ricotta, soft	salmon, sardine, shad,
goat)	tuna)
Cream and milk	Sour cream
Crème fraîche	Stock
Eggs	Water
Fatty meat (filet mignon,	Yogurt

Making Food Luscious, Tender, and Juicy

Along with moisture-rich ingredients, we rely upon certain cooking techniques to make luxurious foods. I can think of five methods that guarantee this trait. Of these, four fall into the category of moist-heat cooking. Moist-heat cooking means that you employ a hot liquid or steam to transfer heat to food in order to cook it. When done correctly, moist-heat cooking methods produce tender, appetizing food.

The fifth technique is a dry-heat method. I will explain later how dry-heat cooking ended up on this list.

Keep in mind that, although I emphasize five cooking methods, you can use other techniques to achieve a sumptuous meal. Baking, roasting, grilling, and broiling can all achieve the desired consistency. Tips for achieving the perfect texture using such techniques are included in the recipes.

METHOD ONE: BOIL OR SIMMER

No matter how new you are to cooking, chances are you have put a pot of salted water on your stove, turned the burner on high, and watched as the water rose to the desired temperature of 212°F. Once you saw steam rising and bubbles dancing across the water's surface, you dropped dry pasta, dried beans, raw meat, or fresh vegetables into the pan. In as little as three minutes or as long as an hour, you had something tasty to eat. Boiling is an easy way to make desiccated foods edible, crisp foods pliable, and raw foods safe and savory.

The difference between boiling and simmering has to do with the amount of bubbles breaking the liquid's surface. When you simmer food, only a few bubbles float to the top. The liquid cooks the food slowly. Simmering is a gentler approach for fragile foods.

You will use boiling and simmering to make such recipes as Summery Bruschetta-Topped Polenta Squares (page 35) and Perfect Pecorino Romano Risotto (page 118).

METHOD TWO: BRAISE OR STEW

As in our first method, braise or stew consists of two closely related techniques of moist-heat cooking. When you braise, you put a vegetable, fish, or meat and a tiny bit of liquid, such as stock or water, into a pan. You then cover the pan and bring the ingredients to a simmer over medium-low heat. The simmering liquid gently cooks the food while the resulting condensation helps to keep the vegetable, fish, or meat moist.

If you want to cook meat and vegetables together with a liquid and keep them all in one pot, you will need to stew them. With stewing you add more liquid plus all the ingredients to

the pot. Both braising and stewing can be done on the stovetop or in the oven.

Lip-Smacking Curried Chickpeas and Potatoes (page 86) involves stewing.

METHOD THREE: STEAM

Another, more delicate, approach to moist-heat cooking is steam. Here the steam from a liquid—water, wine, stock, or broth—and not the boiling liquid itself, cooks the food. In steaming, the food sits on a perforated platform, the steamer, about an inch above the liquid in a pan. The liquid is brought to a simmer. The pan is covered. The steam forms and rises. The food cooks.

Steaming allows foods to keep most of their natural juices, giving us an especially moist repast. Sultry Caribbean Jerk Chicken (page 74) uses a form of steaming.

METHOD FOUR: POACH

There are two types of poaching to consider, deep and shallow. With deep poaching you completely cover food in a liquid that's hot but hasn't reached the boiling point of 212°F. You leave the pot uncovered, watching it to ensure that no bubbles break the surface of the liquid. It sounds easy to do but it does require extra attention. You don't want the liquid to get too hot and your food to boil.

In shallow poaching you rely on both liquid and steam to cook your food. Using a shallow sauté or other pan, you cover the food halfway with a hot liquid. You then place a loose fitting lid on the pan and allow the ingredients to simmer. Steam, which collects under the lid, cooks the part of the food not directly in the liquid. The result is an extremely tender and moist dish.

If you have ever eaten eggs Benedict or enjoyed a particularly juicy chicken or fish dish, you have consumed food that has been poached.

As its name suggests, Velvety Poached Chicken with Tarragon-Shallot Sauce (page 77) employs this technique.

METHOD FIVE: DRY HEAT (FRY)

Technically, frying is considered a dry-heat cooking method. However, because we tend to think of hot oil as a way to trap in moisture and prevent foods from drying out, I have included frying in our list.

Frying in oil makes foods crisp on the outside and tender and juicy within. The trick to creating tasty fried food—as opposed to greasy or gloppy disasters—lies in the cooking temperature. When stir-frying or deep-frying, slowly heat your grapeseed, peanut oil, or canola oil until it reaches 365°F on a deep-fry or candy thermometer. When it reaches the required temperature, lower your food into the hot oil. Once the food has finished frying, remove it from the pan and lay it on clean paper towels to absorb any excess oil. Allow the oil to return to 365°F again before putting your next batch in the pot. Food dropped into oil that hasn't fully heated will end up greasy, largely from all the extra time spent sitting in and absorbing lukewarm oil.

In the following chapters you will either pan-fry, stir-fry, or deep-fry Tantalizing Vegetable Pad Thai (page 84), Crazy Good Corn-Shallot Fritters (page 38), and Six-Napkin Southern Fried Chicken (page 70).

Cooking Tools

The following tools will make life in the kitchen a bit easier. That doesn't mean, though, you should rush out and buy all of these items. In my experience, as long as you own a sharp chef's knife, cutting board, spatula, instant-read thermometer, tongs, measuring spoons and cups, and a good-quality stainless steel frying and/or sauté pan, saucepan, and stockpot, then you possess the tools to cook almost anything. So, until you know for certain that you love to stir-fry or whip up hummus and spreads, borrow a wok or food processor and/or blender from a friend.

Note that a few of these cooking tool items will appear again under Baking Tools. For the recipes featured in *Luscious, Tender, Juicy* you will use the following cooking tools:

- Good-quality 8-inch chef's knife (if possible, go with forged stainless steel)
- Cutting board(s)
- Vegetable peeler (8)
- Box grater
- Citrus zester and/or grater (5)
- Potato ricer (3)
- Rubber or wooden spatula (for sautéing, stirring, and more)
- Metal or nonstick spatula (for removing meat, chicken, and fish from the pan)
- Long-handled, stainless steel tongs (6)
- Round skimmer or large slotted spoon (7)
- Instant-read digital thermometer (4)
- Deep-fry and/or candy thermometer
- Fine-mesh strainer or colander
- Small and large mixing bowls
- Measuring spoons and cups (1)
- 2-quart baking dish with lid
- 3- or 4-quart saucepan with lid
- 3- or 4-quart sauté pan
- 8-quart stockpot with lid
- 12-inch frying pan
- 14-inch wok
- 9-inch loaf pan
- Digital scale (2)
- Kitchen timer
- Food processor or an electric countertop blender
- Baking sheets
- Kebab skewers
- Aluminum foil
- 1-gallon seal-top plastic bags

What about Baked Goods?

If you're like me and you possess a raging sweet tooth, or if you just enjoy a slice of cake or a cookie, you may wonder when we will discuss desserts and sweet baked goods. Have no fear! To-die-for sweets are here!

Okay, they're not actually here in the introduction. You will come across these treats later in the book. There I delve into how to make and keep your cakes, tortes, pies, tarts, breads, buns, cookies, and squares as satiny and delectable as the day you pulled them from the oven.

In the meantime I will pass along a few tips for keeping baked goods moist.

First off, remember that butter adds flavor while oil adds moisture. Generally, we opt for a rich, buttery taste in our baked goods. However, in the case of Aunt Nancy's Stupendous Carrot Cake (page 134), we already have a lot of bold flavors in our batter. With that in mind, instead of butter, we use oil to create the cake's velvety texture.

We have a rule for butter in cookies, too. If you want a cookie with crunch, use more butter and less flour in your dough. However, if you desire a cookie that melts on your tongue, bump

up the amount of flour that you include. A small increase goes a long way toward creating a luscious texture.

Another thing to keep in mind relates to storage. Completely cool your baked goods before storing them. Once they've cooled, put your cookies, breads, bars, pies, and the like in airtight containers. You might think that you have adequately covered them with waxed paper or plastic wrap, but air can still sneak in and damage your treats. Prolonged exposure to air will dry out any baked good.

If you don't plan on icing your cake or cookies right away, wrap them in plastic wrap and cover the wrap with aluminum foil. In addition, and it may sound like overkill, you can tuck these wrapped items into airtight containers, too.

Stash your containers of baked goods in a cool, dark spot. If you plan on icing the treats, do so within 24 hours. For the very best results, consume your sweets within 24 to 72 hours. During this period they are at their freshest and moistest.

More on the reasoning behind these tips later in the book.

Baking Tools

This may seem like a long list of tools to acquire, but chances are you own some of these items already. What you don't own, you can always borrow.

If you do need to purchase any of these items, know that all can be found online or at supermarkets, kitchen stores, and other shops. With the exception of the hand or stand mixer, none are terribly expensive. Several of them you can use not only for sweet but also savory dishes.

For the recipes featured in *Luscious, Tender, Juicy* you will use the following baking tools:

- 8-inch springform pan (1)
- 9-inch springform pan
- 9-by-2-inch round pan
- 8-inch loaf pan
- 9-inch loaf pan
- 9-inch pie pan
- 10-inch fluted tart pan
- 12-cup muffin tin
- 4- or 5-ounce ramekins (8)
- 2-quart baking dish
- Digital scale
- Candy thermometer (3)
- Wire cooling rack(s)
- Baking sheet(s)
- Small disher or cookie dough scoop (5)
- Electric hand mixer or stand mixer
- Mixing bowls
- Measuring spoons and cups
- Rubber spatula or spoon
- Metal spatula (for removing cookies, bars, and the like from their pans)
- Icing spatula or knife (7)
- Whisk
- Rolling pin
- Ceramic or aluminum pie weights or dried beans
- Pastry cutter (6)
- 2½-inch biscuit cutter (4)
- 8-inch chef's knife
- Sharp, thin-bladed knife
- Airtight containers
- Plastic wrap
- Aluminum foil
- Parchment paper
- 9-inch parchment paper rounds (although parchment rounds are quite convenient, you can always use parchment paper from a roll instead) (2)

REGENCY
PARCHMENT ROUNDS
FOR NON-STICK BAKING OF CAKES, PIES & PIZZAS

TAYLOR

Ingredients Source List

FOR LENTILS, HARISSA, SALT, AND HARD-TO-FIND SPICES

Bitterman Salt Co./The Meadow
https://themeadow.com
hello@themeadow.com
805 NW 23rd Avenue
Portland, OR 97210
503-305-3388

Kalustyan's
https://kalustyans.com
123 Lexington Avenue
New York, NY 10016
212-685-3451

Spicewalla
www.spicewallabrand.com
info@spicewallabrand.com
829 Riverside Drive
Suite 110
Asheville, NC 28801
828-417-7010

FOR CRACKED RYE AND FLOUR PRODUCTS

Janie's Mill
www.janiesmill.com
cecilia@janiesmill.com
405 N. 2nd Street
Ashkum, IL 60911
815-953-1073

King Arthur Baking Company
www.kingarthurbaking.com
135 US Route 5 South
Norwich, VT 05055
800-649-3361
For cheeses, oils, and vinegars

FOR CHEESES, OILS, AND VINEGARS

Di Bruno Bros.
https://dibruno.com
930 S. 9th Street
Philadelphia, PA 19147
215-599-1363

Murray's Cheese
www.murrayscheese.com
254 Bleecker Street
New York, NY 10014
888-692-4339

Zabar's
www.zabars.com
info@zabars.com
2245 Broadway (at 80th Street)
New York, NY 10024
212-787-2000

FOR BAKING INGREDIENTS AND SUPPLIES

Fante's
www.fantes.com
mail@fantes.com
1006 S. 9th Street
Philadelphia, PA 19147
215-922-5557

NY Cake
www.nycake.com
118 W. 22nd Street
New York, NY 10010
212-675-2253

Warren Cutlery
https://warrencutlery.com
3584 Route 9G
Rhinebeck, NY 12572
845-876-3444

Zabar's
www.zabars.com
info@zabars.com
2245 Broadway (at 80th Street)
New York, NY 10024
212-787-2000

Two Basic Recipes for Two Basic Doughs

Throughout the cookbook you will find recipes calling for such staples as piecrust and sheets of puff pastry. You can find commercially produced versions in the frozen food section of any market, but these will never taste as good or be as plush as homemade dough.

Although you may have heard tales about how terrifying and labor-intensive making piecrust and puff pastry can be, I can assure you that you do not need to feel intimidated. Sure, making your own dough takes more time than unwrapping and defrosting a mass-produced frozen dough, but, again, homemade will taste and perform better. The time spent will be worth it.

Homemade Piecrust

MAKES ONE 9-INCH PIECRUST

There are countless piecrust recipes in print. I know because I've tried quite a few of them. My go-to recipe, though, comes from old friend and baking enthusiast Elizabeth Theisen, whose mother, Liz Theisen, had passed it down to her.

Liz Theisen had adapted this foolproof recipe from a 1950s Betty Crocker Cookbook. So, with a nod to one of the best-selling cookbooks in American history and to the Theisen family, here's a recipe for a simple piecrust.

INGREDIENTS

1 cup plus 1 tablespoon all-purpose flour, plus more for dusting your work surface

½ teaspoon salt

5½ tablespoons unsalted butter, cold, cut into chunks

4 to 5 tablespoons ice cold water

DIRECTIONS

1. In a large mixing bowl stir together the flour and salt.

2. Using a fork or pastry cutter, cut in the butter a few pieces at a time. (In layman's terms, this means squish or mix the cold butter into the flour so that little nuggets of flour-coated butter form.) Continue until all the butter is incorporated and the mixture resembles small balls or peas.

3. Sprinkle 1 tablespoon of the ice water over the flour mixture and toss to combine. Continue adding the water, up to 5 tablespoons, until all the flour has been moistened and a loose dough has begun to form.

4. Shape the dough into a ball and then flatten it slightly. Wrap it in plastic wrap and refrigerate for 45 minutes.

5. Place the dough on a lightly floured work surface. Using a rolling pin, roll out the dough until it's about 2 inches wider than a 9-inch pie pan. (I just plunk my pie pan on top of the dough and measure it that way.)

6. Gently fold the dough in half and lay it in the pie pan. Unfold and pat the dough into place. The excess dough hanging over the sides of the pan will be your crust's edge. Tuck the extra dough under itself on the rim of the pie pan.

7. If you're filling your piecrust with fruit, add the fruit now. If you intend to use custard or another wet filling, you will need to bake the crust first.

8. Preheat the oven to 375°F. As the oven is heating, prick the crust with a fork so that steam doesn't get trapped beneath it. Weigh down the bottom of the crust with ceramic or aluminum pie weights or dried beans. These weights further prevent bubbles from forming and the crust from puffing up as it bakes.

9. Bake the crust for 15 minutes. Remove the crust from the oven and remove the pie weights. Allow the crust to cool slightly before filling and baking it.

Note: If you use dried beans as your pie weights, you should first line the crust with parchment paper before adding the beans. This makes it easier to take out the beans and also removes the possibility that your crust develops a slight bean taste.

The "Why" and "How" of Blind Baking

Some pie recipes advise you to "blind bake" or prebake your piecrust before filling it. This means that you will briefly bake the crust to set its shape and texture. This step prevents your crust from developing a soggy bottom. It also stops delicate fillings from overbaking.

Depending on the filling and recipe instructions, you will either partially or fully blind bake your piecrust. With partial blind baking, you weight the crust's bottom with pie weights or dried beans and bake the crust until the dough has set, about 15 minutes. The weights are removed. The crust is cooled, filled with its filling, and returned to oven to finish baking. Custards use partial blind baking.

With full blind baking, after baking the crust and removing the weights, you brush the bottom and sides with a whisked egg white. This coating further protects the piecrust from becoming too wet. You then return it to the oven to bake for an additional 5 to 8 minutes, until its edges have begun to brown. Remove the piecrust from the oven and cool it completely before filling and serving. Precooked fillings, such as mousse and cream, require full blind baking.

Homemade Puff Pastry

MAKES ABOUT 2¾ POUNDS OF DOUGH, OR 4 SHEETS

As with piecrusts, I have tried a variety of puff pastry recipes. Some I've sweated over for hours, only to end up with tough or flat pastry dough. Others have been faster to create but offered mixed results. Currently, my go-to recipe for lofty homemade puff pastry comes from The King Arthur Flour Baker's Companion *(The Countryman Press, 2003). Those familiar with the original King Arthur recipe may notice that I have altered it. Feel free to use either version for your puff pastry.*

Remember, to create a good puff pastry, you need a cool room, a flat work surface, and several hours to devote to rolling, folding, turning, and chilling the dough. In the end, you should have roughly 730 microscopically slender layers of dough and 730 layers of fat. It's no wonder that the French call their puff-pastry dessert mille-feuilles, or "a thousand leaves."

INGREDIENTS

FOR THE DOUGH

2½ cups all-purpose flour

1 cup cake flour

2 teaspoons salt

6 tablespoons cold unsalted butter, cut into chunks

1¼ cups cold water

FOR THE BUTTER

1⅔ cups (3 sticks plus 3 tablespoons) unsalted butter, softened

½ cup all-purpose flour

DIRECTIONS

1. Sift the dough flours and salt into a large mixing bowl and then stir to ensure that they're combined.

2. Using a fork or pastry cutter, cut the 6 tablespoons of butter into the flours until they're coarse and crumbly. Pour in the water and stir together. Once the water has been incorporated, use your hands to knead the ingredients for 5 to 8 minutes, until a smooth dough forms.

3. Shape the dough into a rectangle, cover it with plastic wrap and refrigerate for 45 minutes. In the interim, use an electric stand or hand mixer to beat the 1⅔ cups butter and ½ cup flour until smooth, 1 to 2 minutes. Shape the butter into a 5-inch square.

4. Cover the butter with plastic wrap and refrigerate for 30 minutes.

5. Remove the dough from the refrigerator and roll it out into a 10-inch square.

6. Take the butter from the refrigerator, unwrap it and place it at an angle (it should look like a diamond) in the center of the dough.

7. Fold the edges of the dough over the butter so that it resembles an envelope. Using your fingers, seal these edges. If they don't stay closed, brush a small amount of water over the edges and press down again.

8. Now it's time to roll, fold, turn, and chill your dough.

9. On a lightly floured surface, roll out the dough into a large rectangle. Fold the bottom edge of the rectangle up to the center

and the top edge over this fold, so that you have three even layers. Turn the dough 90 degrees to your right, roll it out, and fold it again into three layers, as above. Wrap the dough in waxed paper and refrigerate it for 45 minutes.

10. Repeat this roll-fold-turn-roll-fold-chill process two more times. When you're finished, you will have rolled and turned the dough six times total. After the final chilling, you may either shape the pastry and bake it, or tightly wrap and freeze it for up to 3 months.

A Few Words about Global Cooking and the Recipes in This Cookbook

I come from a long line of travelers and food lovers, so it's no surprise that my recipes highlight some of the best dishes from around the globe. In the late 1800s my maternal great-grandparents journeyed by ship to Europe, Egypt, and the Middle East. At the end of their extensive travels they returned home with precious black-and-white images of dining outdoors at long, white cloth-covered tables while consuming such exotic foods as fresh dates, olives, and preserved lemons. As a child, I studied those faded photos and imagined how otherworldly their meals must have tasted and how extraordinary each adventure must have been.

In the early 20th century my maternal grandfather lived in Mexico where, as a mining and civil engineer, he oversaw silver and gold mines by day. At night he hung out with the locals, eating, drinking, and experiencing life as they did. He, too, left behind photographs as well as letters detailing his time along Mexico's Gulf Coast. He further spurred my interest in experiencing the world.

Because this wanderlust skipped a generation, I feel as though I received a double dose of it, making me the most relentless traveler from my maternal family. To date, I have journeyed through 51 countries and six continents. Wherever I've roamed, I've sought out local chefs and ardent home cooks, worked in their kitchens, and learned how to prepare their countries' specialties. Time spent with these generous, patient artisans has influenced my outlook, my cooking, and my work.

Along with this inclination to travel, I have long been influenced by the communities in which I've lived. Growing up in an ethnically diverse, former steel town north of Pittsburgh, I learned early on about exciting and influential world cuisines. Pasta fagioli, pita, and pierogies all shaped my palate and spurred my interest in global cooking. Friends' parents, neighbors, teachers, and, later, colleagues expanded my culinary interests. I could never eat a piece of honeyed baklava or bowl of savory pho and not ask how it had been made. Whenever I could, I would finagle my way into other people's kitchens and learn firsthand how to craft beautiful holiday breads or perfectly wrapped spring rolls. The same holds true today.

As you read through this book, I hope that you, too, develop an appreciation for global cuisines. I likewise hope that you find inspiration for your cooking and fall in love with delectably moist foods.

Lip-Smacking

Snacks

and

Savory Baked

Goods

THE NEXT TIME YOU HOST A PARTY OR SMALL gathering of friends, skip the bland pretzels, crackers, and chips. Along with being unexciting and so overdone, these dry, salty appetizers tend to make people thirsty. The more your friends drink, the less room they have for your beautifully prepared meal.

Instead of dull, thirst-inducing bites, offer your guests a few succulent, satisfying snacks such as Oh-So-Pleasing Pumpkin Hummus (page 28), Melt-in-Your-Mouth Mushroom Puffs (page 42), and Summery Bruschetta-Topped Polenta Squares (page 35). You'll wow everyone with the moist texture, complex flavors, and overall deliciousness of these treats. Your friends will thank you for ditching the usual, tired offerings and giving them something special to eat.

Along with being luscious and delectable, these snacks and baked goods are easy to make. Beyond a small, inexpensive biscuit cutter (for the Mini-but-Mighty Brie Pies, page 46) and a blender or food processor (for Oh-So-Pleasing Pumpkin Hummus, page 28, and Silken Sardine Spread, page 30), you don't need to track down and borrow or buy any special equipment. Nor do you have to spend hours preparing these hors d'oeuvres. They are quick and simple, the perfect starters for time-pressed hosts and cooks.

Oh-So-Pleasing Pumpkin Hummus

SERVES 2 TO 4

Inspired by the now-shuttered SoHo restaurant Back Forty West, this velvety hummus gets its exceptional creaminess from its star ingredient: pumpkin. Chickpeas still play a role, adding a bit of heartiness to this otherwise light dip. Oh-So-Pleasing Pumpkin Hummus pairs well with toasted baguette, sliced cucumber, pita bread, and pita chips. The savory taste of this hummus makes it a good starter for Buttery Sea Scallops (page 66) and Sizzling Lentil-Stuffed Red Bell Peppers (page 59).

If you're feeling ambitious or have a few too many pumpkins on hand, make this hummus using fresh pumpkin. See the recipe for Homemade Pumpkin Puree for details.

INGREDIENTS

15 ounces (roughly 1½ cups) canned pure pumpkin or fresh pumpkin puree

¾ cup canned chickpeas, rinsed and drained

1 garlic clove

2 tablespoons tahini

¼ teaspoon ground white pepper

¼ teaspoon allspice

½ teaspoon sweet paprika

1 teaspoon salt, plus more if needed

3 tablespoons extra virgin olive oil, plus extra, optional, for garnish

Pinch of ground sumac, optional, for garnish

Pita chips, baguette slices, and/or cucumber slices, optional, for serving

DIRECTIONS

1. In the bowl of a blender or food processor place the pumpkin, chickpeas, garlic, tahini, pepper, allspice, paprika, salt, and olive oil and puree until smooth.

2. Spoon the hummus into a bowl. If desired, sprinkle the top with ground sumac and olive oil. Serve with pita chips, baguette slices, and/or cucumber slices, if desired.

HOMEMADE PUMPKIN PUREE

SERVES 2 TO 4

Feeling ambitious? Just don't like canned fruit and veggies? Take heart! You can make your own pureed pumpkin for this dish.

DIRECTIONS

1. To begin, preheat your oven to 375°F.

2. Slice a medium-sized pumpkin in half from top to bottom and scoop out the seeds.

3. Place the pumpkin halves, cut sides down, on a rimmed baking sheet and sprinkle ½ cup water over each.

4. Put the pan in the preheated oven and roast the pieces until tender. Depending on the size of the pumpkin, this takes between 30 to 60 minutes.

5. Once the halves have cooled to room temperature, scrape the flesh from the skin and place it either in the bowl of a food processor or a regular mixing bowl. Based upon the amount of roasted pumpkin, add several tablespoons of butter—usually 1 tablespoon per 8 ounces of flesh—and process or mash with a big wooden spoon until smooth. There you have it! Pureed pumpkin.

Silken Sardine Spread

MAKES ABOUT 1½ CUPS

I created a version of this spread for my seafood cookbook Fish Market *(Running Press, 2013). I've always loved the silky texture that an oily, omega-3–rich fish like the sardine imparts. Plus, I'm always surprised by how many people marvel that Silken Sardine Spread contains fish. Invariably, after stating how much they like the spread, they say, "You know, it's not the least bit fishy" or "I always thought I hated sardines. Turns out I don't." High praise, indeed!*

After pulsing the ingredients together in a blender or food processor, you can pair this smooth spread with everything from crackers, pita, pretzels, and bread to cucumbers, carrots, spring onions, bell peppers, and more. Silken Sardine Spread goes well with other appetizers such as Divine Danish Brown Bread (page 50), Summery Bruschetta-Topped Polenta Squares (page 35), and Melt-in-Your-Mouth Mushroom Puffs (page 42). It's also a nice starter for Tantalizing Vegetable Pad Thai (page 84), Lavish Lime-Marinated Mackerel Kebabs (page 68), and most other fish or vegetable dishes.

INGREDIENTS

One 8-ounce package cream cheese, at room temperature

One 3.75-ounce can boneless, skinless sardines, drained

3 tablespoons reduced-fat mayonnaise

2 teaspoons freshly squeezed lemon juice

½ teaspoon granulated onion

½ teaspoon sea salt

1 garlic clove, crushed

¼ teaspoon sweet paprika

⅛ teaspoon ground white pepper

Generous pinch of cayenne pepper

DIRECTIONS

Place all the ingredients in the bowl of a food processor or in a medium mixing bowl and process or mash together until the mixture is smooth and well combined. Taste and adjust the seasonings as necessary, then cover and refrigerate until firm, at least 30 minutes. Serve chilled.

School of Omega-3–Rich Fish

Searching for a wholesome, luxurious, omega-3–rich fish? Look no further than sardines. These small, iridescent fish contain large amounts of omega-3 fatty acids, which may lower the risk of cardiovascular diseases and cancers. They are also a good source of protein. Because sardines primarily consume plants, they don't accumulate high levels of mercury that larger, carnivorous fish do.

Beyond their health benefits, sardines woo diners with moist, rich meat reminiscent of hearty tuna. Due to their oily nature, they bump up the amount of moisture in any dish.

Sardines also gain fans with their ability to partner well with a range of ingredients. Eggplants, bell peppers, garlic, and tomatoes; lemons, oranges, and raisins; and herbs such as basil, fennel, parsley, and rosemary all complement the earthy tang of sardines.

Succulent Smoked Salmon Cucumber Rounds

MAKES APPROXIMATELY 36 ROUNDS

Smoked salmon is one of those melt-in-your-mouth foods that needs little else to shine. When you put cucumbers, lemon, cream cheese, and sour cream with this silken smoked fish, you create a marvelously moist offering fit for any party or meal. I like to serve these alongside Tender Zucchini-Basil Pancakes with Crème Fraîche (page 45) and as a cool starter for Sultry Caribbean Jerk Chicken (page 74) and Superb Steak Success Story (page 82).

INGREDIENTS

2 large, unwaxed cucumbers

8 ounces smoked salmon

8 ounces light cream cheese, softened

4 ounces reduced fat sour cream

1 small shallot, diced

Zest of 1 lemon

Juice of ½ lemon

¼ teaspoon sea salt

¼ teaspoon white ground pepper

Sprigs of fresh dill, for serving

DIRECTIONS

1. Cut off the ends of the cucumbers and slice them into ¼-inch-thick rounds. Using a spoon or your knife, gently remove most of the seeds from each slice, leaving about a third of the center intact. Set the slices aside.

2. Place half (4 ounces) of the smoked salmon on a cutting board. Using a sharp knife, dice the salmon and place the small pieces into a bowl.

3. Cut the remaining portion of smoked salmon into 1-inch strips. Place them on a platter or other clean, flat surface.

4. In a medium bowl, using either a heavy spoon or an electric hand mixer, beat together the cream cheese and sour cream until the lumps are gone. Add the diced salmon, shallot, lemon zest and juice, salt, and pepper and stir until well combined.

5. Using a spoon, place equal amounts of filling in the center of each cucumber round. Top the filling with a slice of smoked salmon and sprig of dill. Refrigerate until ready to serve.

Smoked Salmon or Gravlax

These two terms are used interchangeably to describe two different ways of preserving salmon. Smoked salmon, as its name suggests, is raw salmon that has been cured in salt and then smoked in a smokehouse. Born out of necessity, smoking was the means by which medieval Europeans, particularly in Scotland and Ireland, ensured that their bountiful salmon catches would remain edible throughout the year.

Often confused with smoked salmon, gravlax is raw salmon cured in a mixture of salt, sugar, and dill. Gravlax dates back to medieval times when Swedish fishermen would salt and then wrap freshly caught salmon in strips of birch bark. To protect their catches from hungry animals, they would bury the packets of fish in the ground. Along with protecting the salmon, this practice gave the fish its velveteen texture and provided it with its name. In Swedish *grav* means "tomb" or "grave" while *lax* refers to salmon.

As you might expect, gravlax has a mildly salty-sweet flavor, while smoked salmon has a smoky taste. Although either type of cured fish can be used in recipes, I tend to partner smoked salmon with bolder ingredients such as capers, shallots, or red onions; and gravlax with gentler foods such as eggs, bagels, or cream cheese. That way, the delicate gravlax won't be overshadowed by stronger flavors.

Sweet and Shiny Apricot Coins

MAKES 24 COINS

This sweet dish proves that not every appetizer needs to be savory. The soft tang of dried Turkish apricots, the mellowness of lemon-laced mascarpone cheese, and the crunch of candied nuts come together with golden honey to make a fast, easy, and memorable starter. When selecting dried apricots, I always look for Turkish, which seem plumper and moister than California-produced dried apricots. In spite of being dried, Turkish apricots tend to keep their soft, supple texture.

Mascarpone cheese is the sweeter, creamier Italian version of cream cheese. Made with cream, it has a higher fat content than its American counterpart. In spite of its close ties to American-style cream cheese, when I can't find mascarpone, I substitute goat cheese in this recipe. To make the goat cheese more spreadable, I whisk a teaspoon or two of milk into it.

INGREDIENTS

24 dried Turkish apricots

Zest and juice of ½ lemon

3 to 4 tablespoons mascarpone cheese

12 honeyed pecans, walnuts, or almonds, broken in half

Honey, for drizzling over the apricots

DIRECTIONS

1. Place the dried apricots on a decorative serving platter or plate.

2. In a small bowl, stir together the zest, lemon juice, and mascarpone cheese until blended.

3. Using a small knife or spreader, spread equal amounts of cheese over the top of each apricot. Place a pecan half on top of the mascarpone. Repeat for all the apricots.

4. Right before serving, drizzle honey over each of the nut-topped apricots. Serve immediately.

Summery Bruschetta-Topped Polenta Squares

MAKES NINE 2-INCH OR EIGHTEEN 1-INCH SQUARES

There are two simple tricks to making an outstanding polenta. First, pay attention to your pan and how the contents are doing. Second, continually stir the polenta until it has become soft and fairly thick in texture. Do both and you're guaranteed a delicious pot of polenta.

Summery Bruschetta-Topped Polenta Squares can accompany such snacks as Silken Sardine Spread (page 30) and Succulent Smoked Salmon Cucumber Rounds (page 32). They also make a great starter for Sizzling Lentil-Stuffed Red Bell Peppers (page 59), Sultry Caribbean Jerk Chicken (page 74), Luscious Lemon-Garlic Shrimp (page 64), and Buttery Sea Scallops (page 66).

INGREDIENTS

FOR THE POLENTA SQUARES

2 ¾ cups water

1 teaspoon sea salt

½ cup polenta

¼ cup heavy cream

⅔ cup grated Parmesan cheese

FOR THE BRUSCHETTA

4 garlic cloves, minced

3 tablespoons minced fresh basil

1 tablespoon minced flat-leaf parsley

2 pints cherry tomatoes, quartered lengthwise

1 teaspoon sea salt

½ teaspoon freshly ground black pepper

3 tablespoons extra virgin olive oil

2 tablespoons balsamic vinegar

DIRECTIONS

1. Grease an 8-inch square baking dish with olive oil. Set the dish aside.

2. Place the water and salt in a medium, heavy-bottomed saucepan and bring it to a boil over medium-high heat. Whisk in the polenta and reduce the heat to medium low. Simmer for 10 minutes, stirring frequently with a large spoon or spatula. After 10 minutes add the cream and stir to combine.

3. Cook, stirring continually, for 10 minutes, or until the polenta has softened and thickened.

4. Remove the pan from the heat and add the cheese. Whisk the ingredients together until blended.

5. Using a spatula, evenly spread the polenta in the baking dish. Set the dish aside to cool for 10 minutes.

6. Preheat the oven to 325°F.

(Continued)

7. To make the bruschetta, place the garlic, basil, parsley, and cherry tomatoes in a bowl and toss to combine. In a separate bowl, whisk together the salt, pepper, oil, and vinegar. Pour the dressing over the tomato mixture and toss until coated. Allow the bruschetta to marinate for a few minutes while you bake the polenta.

8. Place the baking dish in the oven and bake for 7 to 9 minutes, until warm but not browned. Remove the polenta from the oven.

9. With a sharp knife, slice the polenta into either nine 2-inch or eighteen 1-inch squares. Using a thin, metal spatula, remove the squares and place them on a serving platter. Top the polenta with equal amounts of bruschetta. Serve warm.

Spoon Out a Side of Creamy, Cheesy Polenta

If you've mastered the polenta portion of Summery Bruschetta-Topped Polenta Squares, then you have actually learned two polenta recipes: polenta squares and a creamy, cheesy polenta side dish.

To make the polenta side dish, follow the steps in the polenta squares recipe through the point where you whisk in the cheese. Instead of pouring the polenta into a baking dish, you'll spoon it into a serving bowl or onto dinner plates. Serve creamy, cheesy polenta hot and enjoy!

Crazy Good Corn-Shallot Fritters

MAKES ABOUT TWENTY 2-INCH FRITTERS

If you're the slightest bit health conscious, you can panfry these fritters. To panfry, heat 3 tablespoons of grapeseed oil in a large frying pan over medium-high heat. Add the fritters and cook, turning once, until they become golden brown in color, about 3 to 4 minutes on each side. As with deep-frying, you'll want to cook the fritters in batches, waiting a few minutes between each batch, adding more oil if needed and allowing it to heat up again.

Crazy Good Corn-Shallot Fritters make a tasty starter or side for Six-Napkin Southern Fried Chicken (page 70), Sultry Caribbean Jerk Chicken (page 74), Meatloaf Like Mom Should Have Made (page 80), and Lavish Lime-Marinated Mackerel Kebabs (page 68).

INGREDIENTS

3 cups fresh or frozen corn kernels

Vegetable oil, enough to fill 3 inches of a stockpot or large, deep saucepan

1 medium shallot, minced

¼ cup minced fresh parsley

1 cup all-purpose flour

1 teaspoon baking soda

½ teaspoon sea salt

¼ teaspoon ground white pepper

2 large eggs, whisked

½ cup milk

DIRECTIONS

1. If using frozen corn, bring the kernels to room temperature. Pat them dry with a clean cloth.

2. Pour the vegetable oil into a stockpot or large, deep saucepan. Heat on medium-high until the oil begins to shimmer. If using a deep-fry or candy thermometer to monitor the temperature, the oil should reach 375°F.

3. As the oil is heating, place the corn, shallot, and parsley in a large mixing bowl and toss together.

4. In a separate bowl, whisk together the flour, baking soda, salt, pepper, eggs, and milk.

5. Add the corn mixture to the batter and stir until well combined.

6. Using a tablespoon or disher, scoop out a small amount of fritter batter and gently drop it into the bubbling oil. Repeat for two or three more fritters. Be sure to space out the fritters. You don't want to crowd the pan. Overcrowding drops the oil's temperature too much. The fritters will have to sit in the oil longer and absorb more oil than if they're cooked quickly at the proper temperature. Plus, overcrowding could result in the fritters sticking together or forming one giant fritter.

7. Fry the fritters until golden, 2 to 3 minutes. Place the cooked fritters on clean paper towels to absorb any excess oil. Cover them to keep warm.

8. Allow the oil to heat up to 375°F again and fry another batch of fritters. Repeat the steps until all the fritter batter has been used. Serve hot with the condiment of your choice.

Mouthwatering Harissa-Capped Potato Croquettes

SERVES 6 TO 8

The North African hot pepper condiment harissa spices up mild, creamy potato croquettes. Along with potatoes, as in this recipe, harissa pairs nicely with fish, chicken, eggplant, squash, and zucchini, and it can also be used as a sandwich spread. If you can't find harissa in your local market, you can always whip it up at home. See page 41 for details on homemade harissa.

Along with being a scrumptious appetizer, these croquettes serve as a delicious side for such entrees as Lavish Lime-Marinated Mackerel Kebabs (page 68), Meatloaf Like Mom Should Have Made (page 80), and Six-Napkin Southern Fried Chicken (page 70).

If you don't regularly make mashed potatoes, you will begin by cooking 1¼ pounds of peeled russet potatoes in a pot of boiling, lightly salted water. Once the potatoes are fork-tender, mash them with the back of a large, heavy spoon or squeeze them through a potato ricer. Stir in 2 tablespoons of butter and ⅓ cup of milk. With that, you're ready to follow this recipe to make the croquettes.

INGREDIENTS

3 cups mashed potatoes, at room temperature

1½ tablespoons flat-leaf parsley, minced

½ teaspoon sea salt

¼ teaspoon ground white pepper

1 large egg

1 teaspoon water

1½ cups Panko bread crumbs

Harissa, store-bought or homemade (recipe follows)

DIRECTIONS

1. Preheat the oven to 425°F. Grease a large baking sheet and set aside.

2. Mix the mashed potatoes, parsley, salt, and pepper in a large bowl and set it aside.

3. In a small bowl whisk together the egg and water. Place the bread crumbs on a large plate.

4. Scoop out 1 tablespoon of mashed potato. Using your fingers, shape it into a 1-inch round or oval-shaped croquette. Dip the croquette into the egg wash and then roll it in the bread crumbs. Place it on the baking sheet.

5. Shape the remaining croquettes. Dip each into the egg wash, followed by the bread crumbs, and place it on the baking sheet.

6. Bake the croquettes for 10 minutes. Remove the baking sheet from the oven and turn over the croquettes. Continue baking for another 10 to 12 minutes, until the croquettes have browned and become a bit crusty on the outside.

7. Place the croquettes on a platter. Either spoon a dab of harissa onto each croquette or offer them with a small bowl of harissa. Serve warm.

HOMEMADE HARISSA

MAKES APPROXIMATELY ⅓ CUP

Making your own harissa is a cinch. You will use a food processor, blender, or mortar and pestle and the following ingredients.

INGREDIENTS

12 medium-sized, dried ancho chili peppers, tops and seeds removed

Enough warm water to soak and soften the chili peppers

1 teaspoon cumin seeds

1 teaspoon coriander seeds

5 garlic cloves, peeled

1 tablespoon hot pepper paste

2 tablespoons olive oil

½ teaspoon sea salt

DIRECTIONS

1. To make the harissa, place the peppers in a bowl and cover them with warm water. Allow them to sit for 45 minutes or until soft.

2. As the peppers are soaking, place the cumin and coriander seeds in a small frying pan and toast them over medium heat until golden and aromatic. Remove the pan from the heat, cool the spices, and then grind them in either a spice or coffee grinder or pulverize them with a pestle and mortar.

3. Drain the chilies and place them in the bowl of a food processor or blender or a mortar. Add the garlic and pulse or pound with a pestle until you have a crunchy paste. Add the ground spices, hot pepper paste, olive oil, and salt to the bowl and pulse or pound until combined, about 30 seconds.

4. Remove the harissa from the bowl and spoon it into an airtight container. Pour a thin layer of olive oil over the top of the harissa and close the container. When refrigerated, homemade harissa will keep for up to 2 weeks.

Melt-in-Your-Mouth Mushroom Puffs

MAKES APPROXIMATELY 2½ DOZEN PUFFS

Mushrooms pair with buttery puff pastry in this dish to create velvet-like, bite-sized snacks. Before cooking fresh mushrooms, remember to give each a quick sniff. A sweet, earthy odor should rise from the firm, heavy flesh. Any slimy, foul-smelling ones should be tossed into the trash or compost bin. Once you've sorted out your mushrooms, be sure to brush off each with a damp paper towel before slicing and cooking. Mushrooms consist of roughly 92 percent water. You don't want to add more by drenching them in it.

These mushroom puffs are a great starter for Creamy Caramelized Onion Quiche (page 61), Superb Steak Success Story (page 82), Meatloaf Like Mom Should Have Made (page 80), and Lip-Smacking Curried Chickpeas and Potatoes (page 86).

INGREDIENTS

2 sheets puff pastry, homemade (page 22) or store-bought

Flour, for dusting the work surface

4 tablespoons unsalted butter

20 ounces cremini or white button mushrooms, cleaned and trimmed

1 large shallot, minced

1 teaspoon sea salt

Freshly ground white pepper, to taste

1 tablespoon water

1 large egg, beaten

1 cup grated Gruyère cheese

Several sprigs of fresh flat-leaf parsley, minced

DIRECTIONS

1. If using frozen puff pastry, thaw the pastry sheets according to the manufacturer's instructions.

2. Preheat the oven to 400°F.

3. On a lightly floured work surface, gently roll out the sheets of puff pastry. You want to smooth out the pastry.

4. Using a 2½-inch biscuit cutter, cut out approximately 30 circles. Half will be used as the bottoms of the mushroom puffs. The other half will serve as the tops. Place the bottoms on ungreased baking sheets, spacing them 2 inches apart.

5. Melt the butter in a large frying or sauté pan over medium heat. Add the mushrooms and sauté until slightly softened, 3 to 4 minutes.

6. Add the shallot, salt, and pepper and continue cooking over medium heat until the mushrooms are soft and slightly browned, another 3 to 4 minutes. Remove the pan from the heat.

7. Add the water to the beaten egg and set aside.

8. Place 1 tablespoon of the mushroom filling on the center of each circle. Sprinkle the cheese and parsley over the mushrooms.

9. Taking one of the puff's precut tops, apply the egg wash to the edges. Place the moistened side on top of the mushrooms and press down on the edges to seal the two crusts together. Repeat until all the puffs are assembled.

10. Bake the puffs for approximately 10 to 15 minutes, until they have risen and turned golden brown. For best results, serve immediately.

Tender Zucchini-Basil Pancakes with Crème Fraîche

MAKES TWELVE 3-INCH PANCAKES

Zucchini is another great ingredient for increasing the moisture in a dish. To prevent it from making your pancakes soggy, you'll salt the shredded zucchini; salting will draw out some of the liquid from this water-rich vegetable.

The delicate, sweet flavor of this summer squash pairs well with a variety of herbs. In place of basil you could use fresh mint, marjoram, flat-leaf parsley, or thyme. Each will taste delicious in these pancakes. If you can't track down crème fraîche, you can substitute sour cream in this recipe.

Tender Zucchini-Basil Pancakes with Crème Fraîche go well with other appetizers such as Succulent Smoked Salmon Cucumber Rounds (page 32) and as starters for such mains as Soused Spinach and Tomato-Topped Mushrooms (page 56), Luscious Lemon-Garlic Shrimp (page 64), and Tantalizing Vegetable Pad Thai (page 84).

INGREDIENTS

2 pounds zucchini, peeled and shredded

1 teaspoon sea salt

2 large eggs

½ cup Panko bread crumbs

⅓ cup all-purpose flour

¼ cup grated Parmesan cheese

4 green onions, white and 1 inch of green, diced

3 tablespoons minced fresh basil

¼ teaspoon ground black pepper

2 tablespoons olive oil

4 ounces crème fraîche, for serving

DIRECTIONS

1. Place the shredded zucchini in a strainer or on a plate. Sprinkle half of the salt over the zucchini, toss together, and set it aside for 15 minutes.

2. In a large bowl, whisk together the remaining salt, eggs, bread crumbs, flour, cheese, onions, basil, and black pepper.

3. Drain off the liquid from the zucchini. Place the zucchini on clean towels and, using your hands, wring out any remaining water. Add the zucchini to the batter and stir until well combined.

4. In a large frying pan, heat half of the olive oil over medium heat. When the oil shimmers in the pan, you're ready to cook.

5. Scoop out 2 tablespoons of batter and drop it into the hot oil. Using a spatula or the back of a spoon, flatten out the pancake so that the batter is evenly distributed. You should end up with a pancake that is roughly 3 inches in diameter. Repeat until you have three or four pancakes in your frying pan.

6. Fry the pancakes until golden brown on the bottom, 2 to 3 minutes. Flip over the pancakes and cook until golden, 2 to 3 minutes. Repeat, using the remainder of the olive oil, until all the pancakes have been made.

7. Serve warm with a dollop of crème fraîche on each pancake.

Mini-but-Mighty Brie Pies

MAKES 18 TO 24 MINI PIES

This dish screams lusciousness. You've got buttery puff pastry, creamy Brie cheese, and syrupy honey coming together to create incredibly moist and delectable mouthfuls.

Mini-but-Mighty Brie Pies make a lovely starter for Soused Spinach and Tomato-Topped Mushrooms (page 56), Superb Steak Success Story (page 82), and Sultry Caribbean Jerk Chicken (page 74). For a slightly unorthodox dinner entree, partner them with Satisfying Carrot-Ginger Slaw (page 103), Saucy Italian Bread Salad (page 94), or Refreshing Green Apple and Beet Salad (page 93) and a side of mixed greens.

INGREDIENTS

2 sheets puff pastry, homemade (page 22) or store-bought

Flour, for dusting the work surface

8 ounces Brie cheese, rind removed

¼ cup roughly chopped walnuts or pecans

Ground black pepper, to taste

Honey, for dressing

DIRECTIONS

1. Preheat the oven to 425°F. Grease a 12- or 24-cup miniature muffin pan.

2. Place a sheet of puff pastry on a lightly floured work surface. After dusting the top of the pastry with flour, roll out the pastry into a large rectangle roughly 9 by 12 inches.

3. Using a 2½-inch biscuit cutter, cut out as many crusts as you can from the sheet of pastry. Roll out the other sheet of puff pastry and continue cutting with your biscuit cutter until you have 18 to 24 crusts.

4. Place one crust into each cup of the muffin pan. Pat and smooth out the pastry so that it evenly fills out the cup. Put several pie weights or dried beans inside of each cup.

5. Bake for 12 to 15 minutes, until the dough begins to brown and has puffed up. Don't worry if the pastry has puffed up around the pie weights. After removing the pan from the oven, you will use a spoon to remove the pie weights and push the pastry back so that it has a depression in its center.

6. Reduce the oven temperature to 350°F

7. Place 1 teaspoon of Brie, followed by a sprinkling of walnuts, in the center of each crust.

8. Bake until the Brie has melted and the nuts begin to toast, about 4 to 6 minutes. Remove the pan from the oven and allow the pies to cool for 1 to 2 minutes before placing them on a platter.

9. Repeat the above steps with the remaining crusts and filling.

10. Once all the pies have been baked, sprinkle a small amount of pepper and honey over each. Serve warm.

Finger-Lickin' Fig and Red Onion Pissaladière

SERVES 8

You say "pizza." I say heavenly pissaladière. Hailing from Nice, France, this tender, pizza-like dish traditionally features caramelized onions, olives, and anchovies. Here I've replaced the fish and olives with lush fresh figs and a smidgen of blue cheese. If you can't find fresh figs, you can substitute three dried figs. Just soak them for 15 minutes in ⅓ cup boiling water and 1 tablespoon honey before draining and slicing them.

As this is a heartier appetizer, it goes better with lighter entrees, such as Lavish Lime-Marinated Mackerel Kebabs (page 68). You can also pair it with Saucy Italian Bread Salad (page 94), Tart Cucumber Salad (page 96), or Refreshing Green Apple and Beet Salad (page 93) and serve the pissaladière and salad as your main course.

INGREDIENTS

1 sheet puff pastry, homemade (page 22) or store-bought

Flour, for dusting the work surface

1 tablespoon olive oil

½ small red onion, thinly sliced

⅛ teaspoon salt

3 ripe black Mission or other sweet figs, sliced

1 to 2 ounces Gorgonzola or other blue cheese, crumbled

DIRECTIONS

1. Preheat the oven to 400°F. Roll out the puff pastry and place it on a baking sheet.

2. Heat the olive oil in a small sauté pan over medium heat. Add the onion and sprinkle with the salt. Sauté until just softened, 2 minutes. Remove the pan from the heat.

3. Bake the puff pastry until puffed up and slightly golden, about 10 minutes. Remove the pan from oven and spread the onions and then the fig slices over the pastry. Leave an inch border all the way around. Scatter the cheese crumbles over the onions and figs.

4. Return the pizza to the oven and bake for another 5 minutes, until the cheese has melted and the crust turns golden brown. Slice into equal-sized squares and serve.

A Few Helpful Facts about Figs

When selecting a delicate, fresh fig, look for fruit that feels soft but not squishy. Squishy figs should be avoided. Skip the hard fruit, too. Once figs have been picked, they stop ripening so they won't get softer with time. Avoid any with splits, bruises, black spots, or wrinkles. Lastly, steer clear of oozing fruit. Similar to squishy figs, these are figs that have gone bad.

In terms of flavor, Mission and Adriatic rank as the sweetest figs. Brown Turkey, which looks similar to the dusky Mission, falls into the category of moderately sweet. So, too, does Calimyrna. Kadota is the mildest fig that you'll find at markets. Even so, it is still fairly sweet.

You can store figs in the refrigerator for two to three days. Simply place them on a plate, uncovered, and refrigerate. When you're ready to consume them, rinse and then bring them to room temperature. Being cold dulls their ambrosial flavor.

Divine Danish Brown Bread

MAKES TWO 8-BY-4-INCH LOAVES

Usually you can't tinker with baked goods recipes. This is not the case with Divine Danish Brown Bread. Feel free to eliminate the beer, replacing it with water. While I prefer a mix of flax and sunflower seeds, you could use poppy, sesame, and caraway or just one type of the aforementioned seeds. Although I make this with light rye flour, dark rye would be delicious, too. No matter how you choose to alter the recipe, you should include cracked rye. You can find these cut rye kernels at some specialty markets, but I usually order them online from small, independently owned flour mills.

Divine Danish Brown Bread makes a delicious base for Silken Sardine Spread (page 30). It also goes well with Succulent Smoked Salmon Cucumber Rounds (page 32), Soused Spinach and Tomato-Topped Mushrooms (page 56), Buttery Sea Scallops (page 66), Velvety Poached Chicken with Tarragon-Shallot Sauce (page 77), and Superb Steak Success Story (page 82). For a simple snack serve it with cheese, smoked fish, or preserves. Serve with an array of cheeses, including cheddar, goat, and Manchego, smoked fish, Silken Sardine Spread, or an assortment of sweet preserves or butters.

Note that this is the only appetizer recipe requiring more than 40 minutes of your time. Believe me, this wholesome bread is worth the effort and wait.

INGREDIENTS

FOR THE STARTER

2 cups whole wheat flour

2 cups water

⅛ teaspoon active dry yeast

FOR THE BREAD

1¼ cups starter

2 cups cracked rye

2 cups rye flour

2 cups whole wheat flour

¾ cup roasted sunflower seeds

¼ cup flax seeds

1 tablespoon coarse sea salt

1 cup beer (lager)

2 cups water, plus more if needed

2 tablespoons barley malt syrup

DIRECTIONS

1. To make the starter, mix the flour, water, and yeast in a bowl. Cover the bowl with plastic wrap and allow the mixture to ferment for 5 hours at room temperature. Note that once it's finished fermenting, you can refrigerate the starter for up to 3 days.

2. Measure out 1¼ cups of starter. Place that along with the cracked rye, rye flour, wheat flour, sunflower and flax seeds, salt, beer, 2 cups of water, and barley malt syrup in a large bowl. Mix together until well combined. Cover and allow the dough to rest for 30 minutes.

3. Grease two 8-by-2-inch loaf pans and set aside.

4. After 30 minutes, check the dough's consistency. If it seems overly dry and unyielding, stir in up to ¼ cup of water; you want the dough to be firm but also soft. Using a spatula, spoon equal amounts of dough into each loaf pan. Smooth out the tops so that the dough is distributed evenly. Cover the pans with a clean, damp dishcloth and allow the loaves to rise for 12 hours at room temperature.

5. Preheat the oven to 325°F.

6. Uncover the loaves and, using a toothpick or skewer, poke 20 or so holes, from top to bottom, in each loaf. This will stop the loaves from forming air pockets and, subsequently, holes in the bread.

7. Bake for 1¼ hours, until a firm crust forms on top and the loaves begin to separate from the sides of the pan. Remove and cool the loaves in their pans for 5 minutes before removing and placing them on wire racks to cool completely.

Satiny Rosemary-Stilton Popovers

MAKES 12 POPOVERS

I love marrying the sharp tang of English Stilton blue cheese to the woody flavor of rosemary. If you don't share my passion for this pairing, you can always substitute grated cheddar cheese and chopped thyme in this recipe. To make plain popovers, leave out the cheese and herbs. All versions are tender and delicious!

Serve these popovers as a starter or alongside such entrees as Soused Spinach and Tomato-Filled Mushrooms (page 56), Luscious Lemon-Garlic Shrimp (page 64), Meatloaf Like Mom Should Have Made (page 80), and Superb Steak Success Story (page 82).

INGREDIENTS

1½ tablespoons melted unsalted butter, plus more for greasing pans

3 extra-large eggs, at room temperature

1½ cups milk, at room temperature

1½ cups all-purpose flour, sifted

½ teaspoon sea salt

¼ teaspoon ground white pepper

1 tablespoon minced fresh rosemary

¼ cup crumbled English Stilton or other rich blue cheese

DIRECTIONS

1. Preheat the oven to 425°F.

2. Grease the popover pans with butter. Place in the oven for 2 to 3 minutes to preheat.

3. Whisk together the butter, eggs, milk, flour, salt, pepper, rosemary, and cheese until smooth. Pour the batter into the preheated pans, filling each cup to less than half full. Bake for 25 to 30 minutes, until golden brown and puffy. Serve hot.

The Popover's Past

Inspired by Yorkshire pudding, that puffy mainstay of the British Sunday roast, popovers date back to 19th century America. While British cooks baked Yorkshire pudding in a rectangular pan with a layer of meat drippings, popovers were made without beef fat and baked in individual cups. As a result, instead of a fluffy, soufflé-like dish, American cooks ended up with golden, satiny rolls.

Similar to Yorkshire pudding, popovers consist of eggs, milk, butter, and flour. The ratio of liquid to dry ingredients gives the batter its levity or "popover-ness." In the oven the liquids create steam, which causes the batter to puff up. Tear into a baked popover and you will see a perfectly hollow center, a side effect of all that steam.

Steam also provides these baked goods with their name. As the steam increases, it pops the batter over the sides of each individual baking cup. Hence the name "popover."

Mouthwatering Mains

WONDERING HOW TO MAKE YOUR entrées mouthwateringly delicious? If you flip back to the Introduction, you'll find a section on moist-heat cooking methods as well as a list of inherently moist ingredients. To save you a little time, I will provide a quick recap.

To add or retain moisture in a dish, remember not to cook it beyond the recommended time or temperature. When cooking meats or seafood, periodically check on the internal temperature with a digital, instant-read thermometer. Knowing the internal temperature will stop you from overcooking or undercooking your dish. Remember that overcooking will result in a dry, tough, or burnt entrée. Undercooking will make your food unappetizing and possibly make you and your guests sick.

As you cook, add more liquids or fats when needed or called for. You don't want your food to dry out or burn in the pan. Cover the food with a lid or aluminum foil to stop overbrowning and increase the moisture in the dish. Uncover the food to reduce the risk of sogginess. Use moist-heat cooking methods and moist ingredients to ensure that your food turns out as luxurious as possible. Keep these tips in mind and you can create the most magnificent, finger lickin', lip smackin' meals for your family and friends.

Reading through the following recipes, you may notice pairing advice; these are sides or starters that complement the flavor and texture of the entrée. When matching dishes, I try to strike a balance. If I have a bold or spicy main, such as Sultry Caribbean Jerk Chicken (page 74), I partner it with a milder side, such as Smooth Goat Cheese Mashed Potatoes (page 109), steamed couscous, or rice. If I have a more delicate dish such as Buttery Sea Scallops (page 66) or Velvety Poached Chicken with Tarragon-Shallot Sauce (page 77), I put it with something a bit more complex in flavor and appearance. This could be the colorful Give-Me-More Moroccan Couscous (page 90), Satisfying Carrot-Ginger Slaw (page 103), or Refreshing Green Apple and Beet Salad (page 93). I stay away from marrying spiced to spiced (Soft, Spicy Eggplant, page 98, with Lip-Smacking Curried Chickpeas and Potatoes, page 86) or rich and creamy to rich and creamy (Sensational South Indian Ven Pongal, page 121, with Creamy Caramelized Onion Quiche, page 61). Instead I try to complement the flavor and texture of foods.

Soused Spinach and Tomato-Topped Mushrooms

SERVES 6

Talk about a luscious mouthful! This recipe features moisture-laden portobello mushrooms, juicy tomatoes, and spinach. Just reading the ingredients list makes me want to grab a stack of napkins!

So that this dish doesn't become soggy, be sure to clean the mushrooms with a damp cloth or paper towel. Do not submerge or rinse any mushrooms under water. The mushrooms will absorb the excess liquid. Once they start simmering in the pan, they'll release the extra water, resulting in a longer cooking time and either an overcooked and rubbery or undercooked and soppy main course.

Soused Spinach and Tomato-Topped Mushrooms can be a meal in itself. However, if you crave a heartier dinner, serve this alongside Marvelous Parsnip Mash (page 104) or some cheesy polenta (page 37).

INGREDIENTS

6 portobello mushrooms, wiped cleaned and stems removed

⅓ cup olive oil, plus more for greasing baking dish

¼ cup balsamic vinegar

3 garlic cloves, minced

1 teaspoon dried parsley

1½ teaspoons dried oregano

1 teaspoon freshly ground black pepper

1½ pounds spinach, cooked and strained to remove water

2 cups diced tomatoes, fresh or canned, drained

4 ounces crumbled feta cheese

Salt, to taste

DIRECTIONS

1. Place an oven rack in the oven's top position. Preheat the oven to 350°F.

2. Place the mushrooms smooth side down in a large baking dish.

3. Whisk together the olive oil, vinegar, garlic, parsley, oregano, and pepper. Pour the dressing over the mushrooms and place the dish in the oven.

4. Bake, uncovered, for 10 to 15 minutes. The mushrooms will be soft and slightly browned when finished.

5. Turn off the oven and remove the baking dish. Put the oven broiler on medium.

6. Divide equally the spinach followed by the tomatoes and then the cheese onto each mushroom.

7. Place the dish back in the oven and broil until the cheese is soft and browning, about 1 minute. Remove and season with salt. Serve warm.

Sizzling Lentil-Stuffed Red Bell Peppers

SERVES 4

Every country seems to have a tried-and-true stuffed pepper recipe. In the United States we have filled peppers with meat and other ingredients since at least 1896. This was the year that culinary expert Fannie Farmer and her seminal The Boston Cooking-School Cook Book *published a stuffed pepper recipe.*

Why the world loads bell and other peppers with savory ingredients is no mystery. In addition to being colorful and edible cooking and serving vessels, peppers impart flavor and moisture to whatever is stuffed inside of them. Should you prefer a meat-filled version of this recipe, consult page 60 for Meaty Stuffed Red Bell Peppers.

INGREDIENTS

4 red bell peppers, tops and insides removed

¾ cup red lentils, rinsed, drained, and sorted

3 tablespoons olive oil

1½ tablespoons sherry vinegar

1 teaspoon Dijon mustard

1 teaspoon sea salt

½ teaspoon ground black pepper

¼ cup chopped fresh Italian flat-leaf parsley

1 large shallot, minced

1 large carrot, peeled and diced

⅓ cup chopped walnuts

½ cup grated Locatelli Romano cheese

DIRECTIONS

1. Grease a small baking dish with olive oil.

2. Bring 4 cups of salted water to a boil in a large saucepan. Place the bell peppers on a rack over the pan and steam for 7 to 10 minutes to soften them. Remove the peppers. Using a small, sharp knife, prick a hole in the bottom center of each pepper; this will allow excess liquid to escape and prevent your peppers from becoming mushy on the bottom.

3. Place the peppers in the prepared baking dish. You should have very little, if any space, between the peppers.

4. Add the lentils to the boiling water and cook, uncovered, until tender, about 20 minutes.

5. As the lentils are cooking, whisk together the olive oil, vinegar, mustard, salt, pepper, parsley, and shallot.

6. Preheat the oven to 375°F.

7. Once the lentils have finished cooking, rinse them under cold, running water and then drain.

8. Put the lentils, carrot, walnuts, half the cheese, and the dressing in a large bowl and stir together until well combined. Taste and adjust the seasonings as needed.

9. Spoon equal amounts of filling into each pepper.

10. Bake the filled peppers for 10 minutes. Remove the pan from the oven and sprinkle the remaining cheese over the top of each pepper. Return the pan to the oven and continue to bake for 15 to 20 minutes, until the cheese is somewhat toasted and the peppers are soft and browning slightly. Serve hot.

MEATY STUFFED RED BELL PEPPERS

SERVES 4

To make a meat filling for your Meaty Stuffed Red Bell Peppers, you will need the following ingredients.

INGREDIENTS

2 tablespoons olive oil

½ pound ground beef

½ white onion, minced

2 garlic cloves, minced

1 teaspoon sea salt

½ teaspoon ground black pepper

3 tablespoons chopped fresh Italian flat-leaf parsley

1 teaspoon dried marjoram

2 large eggs, beaten

1 cup diced tomatoes, fresh or canned

½ cup grated Parmesan cheese

DIRECTIONS

1. To make the meat stuffing, heat the olive oil in a frying pan over medium heat. Add the ground beef, onion, garlic, salt, and pepper and sauté for 10 minutes, until the beef is no longer pink.

2. Remove the pan from the heat. Add the parsley, marjoram, eggs, tomatoes, and cheese to the meat. Stir until well combined.

3. At this point you will follow the steps for filling and baking Sizzling Lentil-Stuffed Red Bell Peppers (page 59). As an aside, remember to preheat the oven to 375°F and to grease your baking dish with olive oil. And don't bother to salt the water used to steam your peppers. Salting only pertains to the lentil version of this recipe.

4. At the end of the baking time, check the internal temperature of the filling in each pepper. It should read 160°F on a digital, instant-read thermometer. If it does, the peppers are done cooking. If not, you'll need to return them to the oven to bake a bit longer.

Creamy Caramelized Onion Quiche

SERVES 8

When I hear "quiche," the words decadent and delicious immediately spring to mind. Hailing from France's Alsace-Lorraine region, quiche consists of pastry crust brimming with a luxurious custard of eggs, cheese, cream or milk, and a range of savory ingredients. Slicing into a hot quiche is like slicing into warm butter. It's smooth. It's rich. It's creamy. It's going to melt in your mouth.

All quiches, but especially Creamy Caramelized Onion Quiche, can be served for breakfast or dinner, as an appetizer or a main dish.

INGREDIENTS

One 9-inch piecrust, homemade (page 20) or store-bought deep-dish crust

¼ cup olive oil

2 large yellow onions, peeled, quartered, and thinly sliced

1 teaspoon sea salt

2 tablespoons balsamic vinegar

6 large eggs, at room temperature

2 cups milk, at room temperature

¾ cup grated white cheddar cheese

½ teaspoon dried parsley

Ground black pepper, to taste

DIRECTIONS

1. If you're using a frozen piecrust, defrost it according to the manufacturer's instructions.

2. Lay the piecrust in a 9-inch pie pan and pat into place. Refrigerate the crust until you're ready to fill it.

3. Heat the olive oil in a large sauté or frying pan over medium-high heat. Once the oil begins to shimmer, add the onions. Sprinkle half the salt over the onions and then lower the heat to medium.

4. Cook, stirring periodically, until the onions begin to soften and become translucent, about 10 minutes. Stirring frequently to distribute the heat and remove any onions sticking to the pan, cook for another 15 to 20 minutes. At this point the onions will be very soft and brown in color.

5. Add the balsamic vinegar to the pan and stir the ingredients together. Allow the vinegar to reduce, 3 to 4 minutes, before removing the pan from the heat. Set the pan aside to cool slightly.

6. Preheat the oven to 425°F. Remove the piecrust from the refrigerator. Place a generous handful of pie weights or dried beans on the bottom of the crust.

7. Bake the crust for 10 minutes, until it just begins to brown. Remove the crust from the oven, take out the pie weights and allow the crust to cool.

8. In a large mixing bowl, whisk together the eggs, milk, cheese, parsley, pepper, and remaining salt. Add the cooled onions to the mixture and stir to combine.

9. Put the cooled crust on a large baking sheet. Pour the onion filling into the crust. Place the quiche in the oven. Reduce the temperature to 375°F.

(Continued)

10. Bake, uncovered, for 35 to 45 minutes, checking halfway through the baking time to see if the crust is browning too quickly. If so, tent a large piece of aluminum foil over the quiche. If you own piecrust shields, feel free to use them instead.

11. When the quiche has finished baking, it will be firm on the edges and slightly soft in the middle. Remove it from the oven and allow it to cool slightly. Serve warm or at room temperature.

Caramelized versus Fried Onions. What's the Difference?

When you fry onions, you cook them in a fat, such as butter or vegetable oil, until they're soft and translucent. Depending on the amount of onions that you're frying, the cooking time varies anywhere from 5 to 12 minutes.

When you caramelize onions, you cook them in a fat and keep on cooking them long past the translucent stage. Eventually, the sugar and starch in the onions begin to break down. The onions start to brown. Even then, you keep on cooking, stirring frequently so that the onions don't stick to the pan. When the onions have finished cooking, they will be extremely soft and chocolaty brown and give off a lovely sweet smell.

To deglaze the pan and cap off your caramelized onions, add a few tablespoons of balsamic vinegar and stir until no onions stick to the pan. With caramelizing, the total cooking time can be as little as 25 minutes or as long as an hour.

What's the difference between caramelized and fried onions? Cooking time and the resulting color, texture, and taste, that's what!

Luscious Lemon-Garlic Shrimp

SERVES 6 TO 8

Dappled with shades of pink and sunny yellow, Luscious Lemon-Garlic Shrimp looks dazzling on your dinner plate. Rich with the gentle tang of citrus and garlic, it is an aromatic delight. One bite of tender, flavorful shrimp and you are hooked on this quick and easy seafood dish.

For information on buying and defrosting shrimp, see How to Select and Defrost Shrimp.

INGREDIENTS

¼ cup olive oil

3 garlic cloves, sliced

½ teaspoon sea salt

2 pounds (26 to 30 count) frozen shrimp, defrosted and peeled

Zest of 2 lemons

Juice of 1 lemon

¼ teaspoon ground white pepper

DIRECTIONS

1. In a large sauté or frying pan heat the olive oil over medium-high. Add the garlic and sprinkle the salt over the top. Reduce the heat to medium and sauté until the garlic has softened but not browned, 1 to 2 minutes. Add the shrimp and cook for 3 to 4 minutes, turning the shrimp over once. When finished, the shrimp will be coral in color and begin to curl.

2. Add the lemon zest and juice and pepper and stir to combine. Cook for another 30 seconds. Spoon the shrimp into a large serving bowl or place on individual plates. Serve warm.

How to Select and Defrost Shrimp

When selecting shrimp, skip the soggy shellfish in the supermarket seafood case. Instead, head over to the freezer section and pick up a bag or two of frozen shrimp. Why buy frozen instead of "fresh"? It's simple. Unless you buy live shrimp, what you find at markets are shrimp that were shipped frozen and then defrosted and put on display. I would rather buy frozen shrimp and defrost them right before cooking

Returning from the market with a bag of frozen shrimp, you glance over at that rarely used microwave oven and wonder whether you could pop those iced crustaceans in there, hit the Defrost setting, and let the microwave do its magic. Let me assure, you cannot.

Microwaving robs shrimp of their moisture and nutrients. It also gives them a rubbery texture that no one enjoys.

If you have the time, remove the frozen shrimp from their packaging, put them in a bowl, and place them in the refrigerator to thaw overnight. When you're ready to start cooking, drain, rinse, and peel the shrimp.

If you decided at the last minute to cook that bag of frozen shrimp, put the frozen shrimp in a bowl of cold water and allow them to thaw there. This can take as little as 30 minutes. You may need to change the water once or twice during this period. Otherwise, both the shrimp and the water will become icy. More often than not, I opt for this fast defrosting method.

Buttery Sea Scallops

SERVES 4

Since medieval times, French chefs have incorporated beurre noisette, brown butter, into their cooking. No wonder! Brown butter enlivens dishes with its warm, nutty flavor and fragrance. When paired with sea scallops, it makes these soft, plump bivalves even more succulent.

For information about differentiating between sea and bay scallops and what to look for in a good scallop, see The Scoop on Scallops.

INGREDIENTS

6 tablespoons unsalted butter

12 to 16 sea scallops

Sea salt, to taste

Ground black pepper, to taste

DIRECTIONS

1. Melt 4 tablespoons of the butter in a small saucepan over medium heat. Once the butter has melted, start swirling the pan over the heat. During this time the butter will foam and then slowly settle, 4 to 5 minutes.

2. Continue cooking and swirling the pan for another 2 to 3 minutes. Once the butter turns golden in color and brown specks begin to form, remove the pan from the heat and set it aside.

3. Season the scallops with salt and pepper.

4. Melt the remaining 2 tablespoons of butter in a large frying or sauté pan over medium heat. Once the butter has begun to bubble, add the scallops.

5. Cook for 3 to 4 minutes, until the bottom side has browned. Using a thin spatula or fish turner, gently turn over the scallops and cook until the other side has also browned, 3 to 4 minutes. Remove the scallops from the pan, place on a large plate or platter and cover with a heatproof lid.

6. Reheat the brown butter over medium heat, about 30 seconds.

7. Place equal amounts of scallops on four dinner plates. Drizzle the brown butter over the scallops. Serve immediately.

The Scoop on Scallops

When buying scallops, you have two options—sea or bay. Sea scallops, the larger of the two, range in size from 1½ inches to 9 inches in diameter. Harvested year round, they appear more often in markets than bay scallops. Because of their widespread availability, they are less expensive.

Petite bay scallops grow to roughly ½ inch in diameter. Although smaller and costlier than sea scallops, they are also sweeter. Due to size, cost, and availability, I opt for sea scallops, which are as moist as bay and likewise flavorful.

As you shop for scallops, consider odor, color, and luster. Scallops should smell mildly sweet and not fishy. They should possess a pale pink to light beige hue and a glistening sheen. Unless they've been soaking in a water solution, they should not be bright white. Because scallops absorb liquids, those placed in a water solution will weigh more and, thus, cost more. They will also be a bit flabby in texture.

For the best quality, ask for dry-packed or untreated scallops. These will be moist but not soggy.

Should you buy a bag of frozen scallops, do not employ my thawing trick for shrimp and tumble them into a bowl of cold water to defrost. Remember, scallops absorb liquid. And don't even think about microwaving these delicate bivalves. Like shrimp, they will become rubbery. Instead, put the scallops on a large plate and allow them to defrost overnight in the refrigerator.

As with all seafood, the key to tender, succulent scallops is not to overcook them. Once they have browned on both sides and lost their opaque color, you can plate and serve them. If you own a digital, instant-read thermometer, you can check the scallops' internal temperature to confirm that they're done. The food-safe temperature for seafood is 137°F. Keep in mind that, even after being removed from their heat source, shellfish and fish will continue to cook. Remember to watch the internal temperature closely and don't overcook your scallops.

Lavish Lime-Marinated Mackerel Kebabs

SERVES 4 TO 6

Include omega-3 fatty acid–rich Spanish or king mackerel in a dish and you are destined for a moist meal. Don't despair if you can't find mackerel at your local market. This marinade works beautifully with other oily, meaty fish such as bluefish, cobia, swordfish, and tuna. To ensure that you buy the freshest, most sustainable seafood possible, see Choosing Wholesome, Sustainable Seafood.

Should you buy frozen mackerel (or another type of fish), remember to unwrap the frozen fish, place it on a large plate, and set it in the refrigerator to thaw overnight. Be sure to rinse off the thawed fish before you begin to work with it.

Lavish Lime-Marinated Mackerel Kebabs pair beautifully with such sides as Refreshing Green Apple and Beet Salad (page 93), Summery Bruschetta-Topped Polenta Squares (page 35), and Zesty Zucchini and Tomato Gratin (page 117). Mackerel also partners well with artichokes, bell peppers, lentils, pancetta, and mushrooms.

INGREDIENTS

Zest and juice of 2 limes

3 tablespoons olive oil

1 teaspoon sea salt

½ teaspoon ground black pepper

1-inch piece fresh ginger, peeled and grated

2 tablespoons chopped cilantro leaves

1½ pounds Spanish or king mackerel, cut into 1½-inch cubes

1. In a medium-sized bowl whisk together the lime zest and juice, olive oil, salt, pepper, ginger, and cilantro. Place the mackerel cubes in the marinade and toss to coat. Refrigerate the fish for at least 1 hour. Note that you can marinate it for a shorter amount of time, but the longer it stays in the marinade, the bolder the lime flavor will be.

2. If you're using wooden or bamboo skewers for your kebabs, soak them in water for 30 minutes. This will stop them from burning on the grill.

3. Preheat your grill or grill pan on high.

4. Thread the fish onto the skewers and lay the kebabs either directly on the preheated grill or on a sheet of foil placed on the preheated grill.

5. Brushing the marinade over the kebabs as they cook and turning so that they cook evenly, grill the fish until just cooked through, about 5 minutes. Serve on or off the skewers.

Choosing Wholesome, Sustainable Seafood

Since I frequently cook and write about seafood, readers as well as friends seek me out to ask what type of fish they should buy. Often they preface their question with "I don't usually cook seafood," "I don't want to buy the wrong fish," or "I don't know what's safe for the environment."

I understand the confusion. Navigating the world of sustainable seafood can seem daunting. Today's consumers are expected to know environmentally friendly fishing methods, when to choose wild-caught over farmed fish and vice versa, and which countries and regions employ sustainable aquaculture. That's a lot to consider when dashing to the store to pick up something quick and healthful to cook.

I give the same advice to everyone. First off, shop at a reputable market. If the market's seafood case looks grimy and smells overly fishy, go elsewhere. A good seafood department displays whole fish, fillets, and steaks on fresh ice. A whole fish will have bright eyes and seem lifelike. Fillets and steaks will be glistening and bright, not dull, limp, and browning. Bivalves such as clams and mussels will rest on ice and not in puddles of water. All fish and shellfish will be stored in clean, refrigerated cases.

Secondly, get to know the head of the seafood counter, the fishmonger. If that person doesn't appear knowledgeable or trustworthy, don't buy your seafood there. A well-informed fishmonger can answer all your questions regarding fishing practices and sourcing.

Thirdly, either download the app or carry the wallet-sized seafood guide produced by the Monterey Bay Aquarium Seafood Watch program. You can also consult the Environmental Defense Fund's online Seafood Selector. Eco-ratings change. These organizations stay on top of improving or declining fishing practices and stocks. Along with a respected fishmonger, they will be your best resources for selecting wholesome, sustainable seafood.

Six-Napkin Southern Fried Chicken

SERVES 4 TO 6

Let's set aside all the negative press about frying and think for a moment about what this technique offers in the way of lusciousness. When you fry battered or breaded chicken, you dry out and crisp up the breading, not the meat behind it. Tucked inside this thin layer of crunchy batter, nestled in with its own moisture and/or steam, the chicken remains tender and juicy even after it's fried.

Something to keep in mind when making any chicken dish is that dark meat (thigh, wing, drumstick) contains more fat and, therefore, more moisture than white meat (breast). Dark meat tends to be more flavorful, too.

INGREDIENTS

4-pound combination of boneless chicken breasts, thighs, and legs

1½ cups buttermilk

1 tablespoon salt

1 teaspoon sweet paprika

1 teaspoon granulated onion

1½ teaspoons ground white pepper

2 cups all-purpose flour

1 teaspoon baking soda

½ teaspoon garlic powder

¼ teaspoon cayenne pepper

Vegetable oil, for frying

DIRECTIONS

1. Rinse the chicken pieces under running water and then pat them dry with a clean cloth. Slice the chicken breasts in half lengthwise to allow for faster cooking. Set the chicken aside.

2. In a large bowl stir together the buttermilk and half each of the salt, paprika, granulated onion, and white pepper. Add the chicken and toss the ingredients together to coat.

3. Put the chicken and marinade in one or two large, plastic, sealable bags. Seal the bags and place the chicken in the refrigerator for a minimum of 2, or maximum of 12, hours. During this period shake or squish the chicken in the bags to ensure that the pieces are marinating evenly.

4. To make the coating, whisk together the flour, baking soda, garlic powder, cayenne pepper, and remaining half of the salt, paprika, granulated onion, and pepper. Place the mixture in a large, shallow pan. Set out a large wire cooling rack.

5. When you're almost ready to start frying, remove the chicken from the refrigerator and allow it to come to room temperature. This will help to create a crisp crust and evenly fried chicken.

6. Take a piece of chicken and, after gently shaking off any excess marinade, repeatedly dip it into the flour mixture so that it's evenly coated. If you see any bare spots, dip the chicken again until it is covered completely.

(Continued)

7. Place the breaded chicken on the rack. Repeat these steps for the remaining pieces of chicken, checking to confirm that they are fully coated.

8. Allow the chicken to dry for 10 to 15 minutes.

9. To fry the chicken, you will need a large, heavy bottomed frying pan or cast-iron skillet. Add enough vegetable oil so that it reaches an inch up from the bottom of the pan.

10. Heat the oil on medium-high until its surface shimmers and the temperature reads 350°F on a deep-fry or candy thermometer.

11. Using heatproof tongs, lower the chicken pieces into the oil. Leave some space between each piece so that they cook evenly. Depending on the size of your pan, you may need to fry the chicken in batches.

12. Cover the pan with a lid and allow the chicken to cook for 5 minutes. After 5 minutes remove the lid and check to see if the pieces are browning evenly and that the oil temperature is between 300° and 325°F. If the temperature is lower than this, you will need to raise the heat to reach the desired range.

13. Keeping the lid off, fry the chicken for an additional 10 to 15 minutes, checking and turning the chicken pieces until they are evenly browned. At this point check the internal temperature of the chicken with a digital thermometer. It should read 165°F.

14. Remove the chicken from the pan and place the pieces on a wire cooling rack that you've put on top of foil or a baking sheet. If you have another batch of chicken to fry, place the cooked pieces on the baking sheet and put them in the oven on low.

15. Before serving, blot the pieces with clean towels to absorb any excess oil. Serve warm with lots of napkins.

Keeping It Luscious, Not Greasy

No one wants to see grease pooling beneath a piece of fried chicken. That's messy and unappetizing. To make your fried chicken as tantalizing as possible, follow these few basic tips.

TIP #1: Have your uncooked chicken at room temperature. Room temperature chicken will cook more quickly and evenly. This holds true for other meats and seafood. The reason for this is explained in Tip #2.

TIP #2: Heat your oil to the specified temperature and no more or less. When your battered chicken hits that shimmering oil, it causes the oil's temperature to drop. (As an aside, if your chicken isn't at room temperature, the oil's temperature will plummet even further and take even longer to reheat.)

If the oil isn't hot enough, it will take longer for it to recover from this temperature drop and reach the proper cooking temperature. Your chicken then sits in the oil longer than it should, which, in turn, produces a soggy, rather than crisp, crust. However, if you overheat the oil, the batter and outer part of the chicken will fry too quickly, giving you an unevenly cooked dish.

TIP #3: Know the signs of properly heated oil. If you don't own a deep-fry or candy thermometer, you can still visually gauge the oil's temperature. To do this, dip a small piece or corner of the battered chicken into the hot oil. If the oil bubbles around the chicken and the batter begins to brown in under a minute, you've hit the right temperature. You can begin to fry your chicken.

TIP #4: Don't overcrowd the pan. If you cram too many pieces of chicken into the hot oil, the oil's temperature will drop too much and you'll end up with that soppy crust mentioned in Tip #2. Add only a few pieces and give your chicken space to bubble away in the pan.

TIP #5: Add more oil as needed, being sure to bring the oil back up to the correct temperature. Skim off any leftover bits of batter in the pan.

Sultry Caribbean Jerk Chicken

SERVES 4

As discussed in Six-Napkin Southern Fried Chicken, dark chicken meat (thigh, wing, drumstick) possesses more fat than white meat (breast). As a result, dark meat tends to be more luscious than white meat. However, with jerk chicken you won't have to worry about a lack of moisture. Thanks to the generous marinade and steamy water bath, Sultry Caribbean Jerk Chicken turns out soft and succulent no matter which pieces of chicken you use.

Unfamiliar with a water bath? Also known as a bain-marie, this method prevents food from quickly drying out and encourages gentle, even cooking. With a water bath, generally, a smaller pan cooks inside a larger pan, which contains water. However, for this recipe you simply slide a pan of heated water onto the bottom rack of your preheated oven. Place your jerk chicken on the rack above it, close the oven door, and allow the chicken to cook. The evaporating water keeps the oven temperature consistent, which, in turn, cooks your food at a steady temperature and rate. The result is a tender, juicy dish.

The spiciness of jerk chicken can be balanced out by Smooth Goat Cheese Mashed Potatoes (page 109), Tart Cucumber Salad (page 96), a simple green salad, or steamed rice.

INGREDIENTS

1 tablespoon olive oil

Four 4-ounce chicken breasts

3 tablespoons Homemade Jerk Sauce (recipe follows)

Hot water, enough to halfway fill a baking pan

DIRECTIONS

1. Place the olive oil, chicken breasts, and jerk sauce in a large, plastic, zip-lock bag. Seal the bag and squish the ingredients together until the chicken breasts are fully coated. Put the bag in the refrigerator and allow the chicken to marinate for at least 90 minutes. The longer it marinates, the stronger the dish will be.

2. Preheat the oven to 350°F. Fill a low, rectangular baking dish or pan halfway with hot water and put it on the bottom rack of the oven. This will be your water bath. Lightly grease another baking dish with olive oil.

3. Remove the marinated chicken breasts from the bag and place them in the greased baking dish. Spoon any leftover marinade onto the chicken.

4. Bake for 1 hour or until a digital, instant-read thermometer inserted into the chicken reads 165°F. Remove the chicken from the oven and allow it to sit for 5 minutes before serving.

(Continued)

HOMEMADE JERK SAUCE

MAKES 1⅔ CUPS

Although the ingredients vary from cook to cook, Jamaican jerk sauce typically contains Scotch bonnet or habanero peppers, thyme, garlic, and onion. Some cooks rub this dry mixture directly into meat, poultry, or fish. Others whisk in a liquid such as olive oil or citrus juice and use the jerk as a marinade. I tend to take the wet route, adding white wine vinegar and soy sauce to the mix. If you like a milder marinade, substitute jalapeño for the habanero peppers. Prefer something with a lot of heat? Replace one or two of the jalapeño or habanero peppers with Scotch bonnet.

INGREDIENTS

3 habanero or jalapeño peppers, halved and seeded

4 garlic cloves, halved

1 small white onion, quartered

1 tablespoon plus 1 teaspoon firmly packed light brown sugar

1 tablespoon dried thyme

1 tablespoon ground allspice

1 teaspoon ground nutmeg

1 teaspoon ground cloves

1 teaspoon freshly ground black pepper

1 teaspoon sea salt

½ teaspoon ground cinnamon

2 tablespoons white wine vinegar

2 tablespoons soy sauce

DIRECTIONS

1. Place the peppers, garlic, and onion in the bowl of a food processor or blender and pulse several times to mince the ingredients. Add the brown sugar, thyme, allspice, nutmeg, cloves, pepper, salt, cinnamon, vinegar, and soy sauce and process until well combined, 1 to 2 minutes.

2. At this point you can either use the jerk sauce or put it in an airtight jar and refrigerate it until you're ready to use it.

Velvety Poached Chicken with Tarragon-Shallot Sauce

SERVES 4

Craving a scrumptious entrée? Try poaching your meat or seafood in a stock or other liquid. The combination of gentle simmering and steaming produces a tender, flavorful dish every time.

For this recipe you will need a shallow sauté or other straight-sided pan with just enough space so that the halved chicken breasts don't touch. The amount of liquid that you include will be based on the size of your pan. Note that the liquid should go only halfway up the sides of the chicken breasts. It should not cover them. Remember that you want to poach, and not boil, the chicken. See Perfecting Poaching on page 79 for more information about this technique.

INGREDIENTS

FOR THE CHICKEN

2 tablespoons unsalted butter

1 large shallot, peeled and sliced

1 leek, cleaned and chopped

1 garlic clove, chopped

2 celery stalks, chopped

2 or 3 sprigs fresh tarragon

2 or 3 sprigs fresh flat-leaf parsley

4 (about 1½ pounds) skinless, boneless chicken breasts

Sea salt, to taste

Ground white pepper, to taste

Chicken stock, enough to reach halfway up the sides of the chicken breasts

FOR THE SAUCE

Stock from the baking pan

1 small shallot, minced

⅓ cup chopped fresh tarragon

Sea salt, to taste

Ground white pepper, to taste

2 to 3 tablespoons heavy cream

DIRECTIONS

1. Melt the butter in a small frying pan. Add the shallot, leeks, garlic, and celery and sauté until slightly translucent, 7 to 9 minutes. Remove the pan from the heat and scrape the vegetables into your sauté or straight-sided pan. Lay the sprigs of tarragon and parsley on top of your sautéed vegetables.

2. Place the chicken breasts on top of the herbs and vegetables. Season them, to taste, with salt and pepper.

3. Pour in enough stock so that it reaches halfway up the sides of the chicken breasts. Bring the ingredients to a simmer over medium heat. Once you see bubbles forming in the stock, reduce the heat to medium-low and place a loose-fitting lid over the pan.

4. Simmer the ingredients for 12 to 18 minutes, until the chicken no longer appears pink and its internal temperature reads 165°F on an instant-read digital thermometer. Remove the chicken breasts, place them on a platter and cover them to keep them warm.

(Continued)

LUSCIOUS, TENDER, JUICY

5. To make the sauce, use a fine-mesh strainer or colander to strain the solids from the stock. Keep the poaching liquid but discard the solids.

6. Pour the liquid back into the pan and bring it to a boil over medium-high heat. Add the shallot and allow the liquid to reduce by at least 50 percent. At this point reduce the temperature to low, add the chopped tarragon and stir to combine. Taste and add salt and pepper if needed.

7. Stir in 2 tablespoons heavy cream. If the sauce appears too thick, add another tablespoon of cream and stir to combine. Turn off the heat and get ready to plate your poached chicken.

8. Place the chicken on four dinner plates. Spoon equal amounts of sauce over each and serve hot.

Perfecting Poaching

To poach food, you cook it in a simmering liquid. In some instances you use both the hot liquid and the steam that it produces to cook your dish. Once the food has reached the required temperature (165°F for chicken; 137°F for seafood), you remove it from the pan and cover it to keep it warm. You then reduce the liquid to make a flavorful sauce for your exceedingly soft, moist entrée.

In poaching you want to simmer, not boil, the food. When measured with a thermometer, the liquid's temperature should range between 160° and 185°F. If it goes higher than this, lower the burner temperature or remove the lid from the pan so that the temperature drops and the liquid and food don't boil. Boiling cooks the food too quickly.

You should poach your poultry, seafood, or vegetables until just done. Don't overcook them. The resulting foods should be moist and tender, not dry or mushy and breaking apart.

The food that you poach should be naturally soft and not need to be tenderized. Poultry, fish, shellfish, and beef tenderloin all do well when poached. Tough cuts of meat, such as chuck roast, require higher temperatures and longer cooking times than poaching provides.

When working with fragile food, such as fish, wrap it in cheesecloth before placing it in the pan. This helps the food to retain its shape and stops it from falling apart during cooking.

Be sure to add herbs, spices, vegetables, wine, and/or citrus juice to your poaching liquid. Generally, the poaching liquid also serves as the base for the sauce. If you start out with a flavorful poaching liquid, you'll end up with a delicious sauce.

Meatloaf Like Mom Should Have Made

SERVES 6 TO 8

A quintessential comfort food, meatloaf has fed the masses since Roman times. As a kid, I was part of those masses, consuming countless variations. Every friend's family had its own special recipe. Even my mom, who usually made dried-out dinners, had a tasty take on this classic. She included an array of moisture-rich ingredients, such as mushrooms, eggs, and cheese. She also baked it in a loaf pan, which helped to keep it moist. To top off her masterpiece, she blanketed it with ketchup, followed by strips of streaky bacon. Savory and somewhat greasy, her meatloaf seemed spectacular to me. Today it seems far too salty and oily. Even so, it did inspire the title of this recipe.

When selecting ground beef, keep in mind that ground chuck will be the fattiest and ground round the leanest. I go with the midrange and opt for ground sirloin.

INGREDIENTS

1½ pounds ground sirloin or other ground beef

1 cup diced white onion

1 cup Panko bread crumbs

⅔ cup white button mushrooms, cleaned, minced, and sautéed

⅔ cup grated Parmesan cheese

½ cup ketchup

¼ cup fresh flat-leaf parsley, minced

2 large eggs, whisked

2 teaspoons Worcestershire sauce

½ teaspoon dried oregano

½ teaspoon ground black pepper

1 garlic clove, minced

¼ teaspoon sea salt

DIRECTIONS

1. Preheat the oven to 350°F. Grease a 9-by-5-inch or 8-cup loaf pan.

2. Place all the ingredients in a large bowl. Using your hands or a large, sturdy spatula, mix the ingredients until well combined. Evenly spread the mixture in the greased pan.

3. Set the loaf pan on the center of a baking sheet and insert this into the oven. Bake, uncovered for roughly 60 minutes. When the meatloaf is done, it will be firm to the touch and no longer cling to the sides of the pan. A digital thermometer inserted into the center of the loaf will read 160°F.

4. Drain off any excess fat from the meatloaf. Allow it to cool for 10 minutes before slicing and serving.

Superb Steak Success Story

SERVES 6

I grew up in a household where meats prepared medium or even medium-well were an anathema. Fearing foodborne illnesses and also not enjoying cooking, my mother roasted, grilled, and broiled meats until not a drop of moisture remained. When sliced and placed on a serving platter, her T-bones and strip steaks resembled leathery jerky or, in the case of filet mignon, oversized charcoal briquettes. What could have been scrumptious steak dinners ended up being chewy, thirst-inducing disappointments.

To avoid dissatisfying dinners like these, remember to cook your meat until it reaches the specified temperature. Don't overcook or cook at too high a temperature. Use the correct size of pan, one that just holds your cut of meat. If the pan is too big, the cooking liquids will burn off and your meat could dry out. Speaking of cooking liquids, for a juicer, more tender and flavorful meat, consider marinating it. You can also dress your filets in a sauce, which is what I do here. Sauce adds a bit more flavor and complexity to this already moist, delicious meal.

INGREDIENTS

FOR THE MUSHROOM SAUCE

2 tablespoons unsalted butter

8 ounces white button mushrooms, cleaned and sliced

½ teaspoon sea salt, plus more to taste

1 garlic clove, minced

⅔ cup chicken stock

½ teaspoon dried parsley

1 to 2 tablespoons all-purpose flour

FOR THE FILET

2 tablespoons olive oil

Four 6-ounce filet mignons

1 teaspoon sea salt

1 teaspoon ground black pepper

2 tablespoons unsalted butter

Mushroom sauce

DIRECTIONS

1. Preheat the oven to 400°F.

2. To make the mushroom sauce, in a medium sauté or frying pan, melt the butter over medium heat. Add the mushrooms and salt and toss to combine. Cook, stirring occasionally, for 2 to 3 minutes, until the mushrooms begin to release some of their liquid.

3. Add the garlic and stir to combine. Continue cooking for 2 to 3 minutes, until most of the liquid has evaporated. At this point add the chicken stock and parsley and simmer for 2 minutes.

4. Sift 1 tablespoon of flour over the sauce and stir until well combined. If you prefer a thicker sauce, sift in another tablespoon of flour and stir. Otherwise, remove the pan from the burner and cover.

5. To cook the filets, pour the olive oil into a large, oven-safe frying pan. Heat on medium-high until the oil begins shimmer.

6. Season the filets with equal amounts of salt and pepper.

7. Put the filets in the pan and cook for 3 to 5 minutes, until the filets are seared on one side.

8. Add the butter to the pan and turn over the filets. Cook, basting the filets with butter, for another 3 to 5 minutes, until the steaks are browned and seared on both sides.

9. Remove the pan from the burner and insert it into the preheated oven.

10. If you want your filets cooked medium (145°F), leave them in the oven for 4 to 6 minutes, checking the temperature with a digital, instant-read thermometer to ensure proper cooking time. For medium-well, leave them in another minute or so until the temperature reads 150°F when probed with an instant-read thermometer. For well done, the internal temperature should be 160°F.

11. Remove the filets from the oven and allow them to rest for 5 minutes. During this time reheat the mushroom sauce on low heat.

12. Plate the filets and spoon equal amounts of the mushroom sauce over each. Serve immediately.

Tantalizing Vegetable Pad Thai

SERVES 2

It took a trip to Chiang Mai, Thailand, and a day spent cooking with a local chef for me to learn how to make a moist and delectable pad thai. Fortunately, you don't have to fly to Asia to master this dish. All the tips you need are right here!

If you own a wok, use it to stir-fry the ingredients. Otherwise, a heavy, well-oiled sauté or frying pan will do the trick. Never made a stir-fry? Check out Moist, Not Soupy, Stir-Fries. There you will find suggestions for stir-frying like the pros. Note, too, that if you leave out the fish sauce, this pad thai becomes a delicious meal for your vegetarian friends.

INGREDIENTS

2 teaspoons grapeseed or canola oil

1 tablespoon tamarind paste

1 tablespoon water

1½ tablespoons traditional or vegan fish sauce

2 teaspoons granulated sugar

1 large shallot, diced

2 teaspoons preserved sweet radish, rinsed and minced

4 to 5 ounces firm tofu, diced

Generous handful of rice noodles, soaked in warm water for 5 minutes to soften

1 small yellow squash, diced

2 spring onions, whites sliced and greens cut into 2-inch long matchsticks

1 small carrot, peeled and cut into 2-inch long matchsticks

Handful of bean sprouts

2 tablespoons chopped roasted peanuts

1 teaspoon chili powder

2 lime wedges

1. Heat the wok over medium-high heat. Add the oil and heat until almost smoking.

2. As the oil is heating, whisk together the tamarind paste, water, fish sauce, and sugar in a small saucepan over medium heat until the sugar has dissolved, 1 to 2 minutes. Remove the saucepan from the heat and set aside.

3. Add the shallot to the wok and stir-fry for 1 minute before adding the preserved radish and tofu. Stir-fry for 30 to 60 seconds before adding the rice noodles and a smidgen of water. You want the noodles to be soft but not soggy. Cook for 1 minute and then add the tamarind-fish sauce.

4. Simmer the ingredients for another 1 to 2 minutes before adding the squash. Cook for 30 seconds and then add the spring onions, carrots, and most of the bean sprouts. Cook for another 30 seconds or until the sprouts and spring onions look slightly wilted. Remove the pan from the heat.

5. Place equal amounts of chopped peanuts and chili powder on two plates. Divide the pad thai evenly between the plates and sprinkle the remaining bean sprouts over each. Place a lime wedge next to the pad thai and serve hot.

Moist, Not Soupy, Stir-Fries

The first time I made a stir-fry, I ended up with a soupy mess. I hadn't made the wok or the oil in it hot enough. I hadn't cut my vegetables into small chunks. What I had done was cook the veggies too long in oil that wasn't heated properly. Instead of crisp and glossy, the vegetables turned out floppy. In an attempt to make the stir-fry taste good, if not look good, I smothered it with soy sauce. The result? I had a puddle of limp, salty vegetables pooling on my dinner plate. Talk about a food fail.

Thankfully, I learned from my stir-frying mistakes. You can, too. To make an appetizing stir-fry, you should slice your vegetables and meat, poultry, or fish into slender, bite-sized pieces. The stir-fry ingredients must cook quickly and evenly. This is why small is best.

Once you have prepared your ingredients, heat your wok or large, heavy-bottomed frying pan on medium-high. You want to see heat rising from the pan and the pan beginning to smoke. At this point add your oil. Tip the pan and swirl around the oil so that it's evenly distributed.

After coating the pan with oil, you can begin to follow your stir-fry recipe. Remember to keep the ingredients moving in the pan—they call it "stir" frying for a reason—and that it is better to undercook than overcook. You can always heat the stir-fry a smidgen longer at the end, but, once the dish is overcooked, you either have to eat it as is or start over.

Lip-Smacking Curried Chickpeas and Potatoes

SERVES 4

Curry is one of those inherently luxurious meals. The word is derived from the Tamil word for spiced sauce, kari, and the dish itself consists of vegetables, lentils, meats, or seafood simmered in a seasoned gravy until tender and aromatic. Traditionally served alongside or over rice, the dish brims with moisture and spice.

Because I find Lip-Smacking Curried Chickpeas and Potatoes so filling, I break with the traditional, hearty rice pairing. Instead I spoon it over plain, fluffy couscous. Feel free to try it with either side.

INGREDIENTS

3 tablespoons olive oil

1 medium white onion, diced

2 garlic cloves, minced

½ teaspoon sea salt

1½ pounds Russet potatoes, peeled and cubed

One 15-ounce can chickpeas, drained and rinsed

2 teaspoons curry powder

½ teaspoon ground cumin

¼ teaspoon ground cinnamon

⅛ teaspoon ground nutmeg

2 teaspoons lemon juice

¼ cup tomato juice (if using canned tomatoes, the liquid from the can is fine)

½ cup diced tomatoes

⅔ cup water, plus more as needed

Steamed couscous or Basmati rice, optional, for serving

DIRECTIONS

1. Heat half of the olive oil in a large sauté pan over medium heat. Add the onion, garlic, and salt and sauté until softened but not browned, 2 to 3 minutes.

2. Add the remaining olive oil and potatoes and stir to combine. Cook for 5 minutes, stirring occasionally to stop the potatoes from sticking to the pan.

3. Add the chickpeas, curry powder, cumin, cinnamon, nutmeg, lemon juice, tomato juice, tomatoes, and water and stir to combine. Place a lid over the sauté pan and lower the heat to medium-low. Allow the ingredients to simmer until the potatoes have softened, 15 to 20 minutes, stirring and adding more water as needed. When finished, the potatoes will be soft but not mushy and the liquid will have reduced to a thick sauce.

4. Serve hot with the optional steamed couscous or rice.

Succulent
Sides

OFTEN, WHEN WE THINK ABOUT LUXURIANT food, we imagine juicy entrees or gooey desserts. Yet, by fixating on meats and treats, we overlook an assortment of intrinsically lush dishes. Consider that bowl of velvet-like mashed potatoes on your holiday table or those succulent sautéed mushrooms accompanying your steak. When prepared correctly, these sides are as sumptuous as the main dishes with which they're served.

In this chapter we will look at sides that feature naturally moist ingredients, including apples, cucumbers, bell peppers, mushrooms, and tomatoes. A more detailed list of moisture-rich ingredients appears in the Introduction.

We will also see how, with the right cooking technique, dry ingredients can be transformed into satiny foods. Couscous, Arborio rice, and moong dal all get a chance to dazzle us with their softer sides.

The following recipes complement the entrées in the second chapter, Mouthwatering Mains. When two sides are partnered together, many become a satisfying, vegetable-focused meal. In the past I've paired Give-Me-More Moroccan Couscous (page 90) with Soft, Spicy Eggplant (page 98); Saucy Italian Bread Salad (page 94) with Zesty Zucchini and Tomato Gratin (page 117); and Exquisite European-Style Sautéed Mushrooms (page 113) with Marvelous Parsnip Mash (page 104). These delectable duos never leave me hungry.

A few sides, such as Perfect Pecorino Romano Risotto (page 118) and Sensational South Indian Ven Pongal (page 121), I've served on their own. Moist and rich, they provide a pleasant change from the usual one-dish dinners of pasta or soup.

Give-Me-More Moroccan Couscous

SERVES 6 TO 8

A staple of North African cuisine, couscous is traditionally cooked by steam in a perforated, two-tiered pot known as a couscoussier. Although I own this tool—I picked one up at a Marrakesh market, stuffed it into our cramped rental car, and hauled it over the Atlas Mountains to the Moroccan desert, and, ultimately, back home—it now sits untouched. Instead of using it, I simply tumble the tiny balls of dried dough into boiling hot water and allow them to steep. Made from whole grain semolina, cooked couscous has a toothsome texture. It acts as rice would, as a side or main ingredient in salads, stews, and desserts.

Give-Me-More Moroccan Couscous honors my well-traveled, now neglected couscoussier and the luscious, aromatic food that it creates. As mentioned in this chapter's introduction, this hearty side tastes fantastic with Soft, Spicy Eggplant (page 98). It also complements such mains as Buttery Sea Scallops (page 66), Sultry Caribbean Jerk Chicken (page 74), and the meat version of Sizzling Lentil-Stuffed Red Bell Peppers (page 59).

INGREDIENTS

8 ounces pearl couscous

One 15-ounce can of chopped tomatoes, drained, reserving 2 tablespoons of the liquid for the dressing

2 red bell peppers, diced

2 scallions, white and 1-inch green, minced

1 cucumber, peeled, seeded, quartered, and diced

3 tablespoons Moroccan or oil-cured black olives, chopped

1 cup chickpeas

¼ cup freshly squeezed lemon juice

¼ cup olive oil

1 teaspoon ground cumin

½ teaspoon curry powder

¼ teaspoon cayenne pepper

Pinch of saffron threads, optional

DIRECTIONS

1. Cook the couscous according to the manufacturer's instructions. Place the cooked couscous in a large bowl.

2. Add the tomatoes, peppers, scallions, cucumber, olives, and chickpeas to the couscous. Toss to combine.

3. In a small bowl whisk together the lemon juice, olive oil, reserved tomato juice, cumin, curry powder, cayenne pepper, and optional saffron. Pour the dressing over the couscous. Stir until evenly distributed.

4. Refrigerate the couscous for at least 1 hour so that the salad can absorb the dressing. Serve cold or at room temperature.

Refreshing Green Apple and Beet Salad

SERVES 6

Inspired by the Scandinavian dish known as sillsallad, this tangy salad features a shockingly hot pink hue and two moisture powerhouses, beets and apples. Refreshing Green Apple and Beet Salad pairs especially well with seafood dishes, including Luscious Lemon-Garlic Shrimp (page 64) and Buttery Sea Scallops (page 66).

INGREDIENTS

3 cups (about 1¾ pounds) cooked red beets, chilled and cubed

¼ cup diced yellow or sweet onion

2 large Granny Smith apples, peeled, cored, and chopped

1 tablespoon plus 1 teaspoon minced fresh tarragon

1 tablespoon minced fresh flat-leaf parsley

3 tablespoons cider vinegar

4 tablespoons extra virgin olive oil

1 teaspoon granulated sugar

Sea salt, to taste

DIRECTIONS

1. In a mixing bowl toss together the beets, onion, and apples.

2. In a small bowl whisk together the tarragon, parsley, vinegar, oil, and sugar. Pour the dressing over the salad and toss to coat.

3. Cover the salad with plastic wrap and refrigerate until chilled.

4. Before serving, add salt, to taste.

Saucy Italian Bread Salad (Panzanella)

SERVES 4 TO 6

Traditionally, cooks would begin this Tuscan salad by soaking slices of bread in water. After squeezing out the water, they would rip the bread into bite-sized pieces and mix it with chopped tomatoes, onions, basil, olive oil, and vinegar. Here I omit the water and include a few extras, such as green and red peppers, garlic, olives, and parsley. While I use the lighter white balsamic vinegar in my panzanella, feel free to substitute red wine or balsamic vinegar. Also, if you can't find Italian bread cubes, you can make your own by cutting a half to full loaf of Italian bread into 1-inch cubes.

INGREDIENTS

4 cups Italian bread cubes

2 cucumbers, peeled, seeded, and chopped

3 large ripe tomatoes, sliced into ½-inch cubes

1 red bell pepper, seeded and chopped

1 green bell pepper, seeded and chopped

2 garlic cloves, minced

1 small white onion, diced

½ cup pitted Kalamata olives, sliced in half

⅓ cup fresh chopped basil

⅓ cup fresh chopped flat-leaf parsley

¼ cup extra virgin olive oil

¼ cup white balsamic vinegar

1 teaspoon sea salt

½ teaspoon ground black pepper

DIRECTIONS

1. Preheat the oven to 350°F. Put the bread cubes on a baking sheet. Toast for 6 to 10 minutes, turning over the bread halfway through the baking time so that both sides get toasted and become firm. Remove the bread from the oven and set aside.

2. Place the cucumbers, tomatoes, peppers, garlic, onion, olives, basil, and parsley in a large bowl and toss to combine.

3. In a small bowl whisk together the oil, vinegar, salt, and pepper. Pour the dressing over the salad and toss to combine.

4. About 30 minutes before serving, add the toasted bread cubes. Toss the ingredients together, making sure that all the bread gets doused with dressing.

Tart Cucumber Salad

SERVES 4 TO 6

Tart Cucumber Salad is the ideal dish for cooling off on a hot summer night, or for brightening a drab winter day. Easy to make, it's packed with refreshing flavors. It goes well with a variety of dishes, including Sizzling Lentil-Stuffed Red Bell Peppers (page 59), Sultry Caribbean Jerk Chicken (page 74), and Superb Steak Success Story (page 82).

If you plan on serving this in a large, shared bowl, be sure to drain off most of the marinade first.

INGREDIENTS

⅓ cup water

⅓ cup cider vinegar

¼ cup granulated sugar

1½ teaspoons coarse sea salt

¾ teaspoon ground black pepper

2 medium cucumbers

2 cups diced honeydew melon

1 spring onion, white and 1-inch green, minced

3 tablespoons roughly chopped fresh basil

DIRECTIONS

1. Place the water, vinegar, sugar, salt, and pepper in a saucepan and bring to a boil over medium heat. As the marinade is heating, halve and then slice the cucumbers so that the slices are $^1/_8$-inch thick. You want them to be thin but not see-through thin. Place them in a large, shallow bowl.

2. Pour the hot liquid over the cucumbers. Allow the ingredients to cool to room temperature.

3. Place the cucumbers and liquid in a large bowl. Add the honeydew, spring onion, and basil and toss to combine. Refrigerate for 1 hour before serving.

Working with Watery Veggies

As much as I like moist, soft foods, I don't want to eat something that's slumped in a puddle of its own juices or turned to mush on my plate. With that in mind, when working with water-laden vegetables, including eggplant and zucchini, I normally cut and lightly salt them. I then allow the veggies to set for a minimum of 15 minutes on a plate, in a colander, on clean towels, or on a cooling rack. During this time the salt draws the excess liquid out of the vegetables. Before cooking with them, I wipe off the extra water and salt.

This releasing of liquid is why some recipes suggest salting onions before frying them. Salted onions give off moisture, which, in turn, permits them to cook and brown more evenly. It also stops them from sticking to the hot pan.

Along with containing ample amounts of liquid, some vegetables absorb them. For spongelike ingredients such as mushrooms, I ditch my usual cleaning technique of scrubbing under running water. Instead, I wet a clean cloth with warm water and carefully wipe the surface of each mushroom. By minimizing its contact with water, the mushroom's ability to take on more moisture is reduced.

Soft, Spicy Eggplant

SERVES 4

This is one of those special bonus recipes—one recipe gives you two different dishes. Near the end of the recipe you have the option of serving slices of Soft, Spicy Eggplant or, after removing the eggplant from the oven, roughly mashing the slices with a spoon and offering a mash. In the latter form, the mash works as both a side dish and a dip for pita or sliced baguette.

When preparing eggplant and other juicy vegetables, I usually slice and then sprinkle them with salt to draw out the excess moisture before moving on to cooking with them. However, because I want my Soft, Spicy Eggplant to be as luscious as possible, I omit that step in this recipe. If you're a fan of leaving skins on vegetables, feel free not to peel the eggplant.

INGREDIENTS

Canola or grapeseed oil, for greasing the baking sheet

2 pounds eggplant, peeled, halved, and cut into 1-inch slices

2 garlic cloves, minced

1 small yellow onion, diced

½ cup extra virgin olive oil

½ cup fresh flat-leaf parsley

½ teaspoon chili powder

¼ teaspoon cayenne pepper

Sea salt, to taste

DIRECTIONS

1. Preheat the oven to 400°F. Lightly spray or brush a large baking sheet with canola or grapeseed oil.

2. Combine the eggplant, garlic, and onion in a mixing bowl.

3. In a small bowl whisk together the oil, half of the parsley, chili powder, cayenne pepper, and salt. Pour the olive oil mixture over the eggplant and toss to coat.

4. Spread the sliced eggplant in a single layer over the prepared baking sheet.

5. Bake for 35 to 40 minutes, until the eggplant feels very soft when probed with a fork. Remove the sheet from the oven.

6. Arrange the eggplant on a serving platter or individual plates, sprinkle the remaining parsley over the slices, and serve. Or you could turn this into a velvety eggplant mash.

7. To make the mash, place the eggplant in a large bowl. Using the back of a serving spoon or spatula, roughly mash the ingredients. Add the remaining parsley and toss to combine. Taste and add more salt if needed. Serve warm or cold.

Glossy Grilled Tomatoes and Feta

SERVES 2 TO 4

I love how grilling releases the juices from the tomatoes and feta and allows their flavors to meld. If you don't have access to an outdoor grill, you can make this dish on your stove with a grill pan. Just use a large lid to cover the tomatoes.

Easy yet so delicious, Glossy Grilled Tomatoes and Feta goes well with Buttery Sea Scallops (page 66), Sultry Caribbean Jerk Chicken (page 74), Meatloaf Like Mom Should Have Made (page 80), and Superb Steak Success Story (page 82). I've been known to spread a layer of creamy, cheesy polenta or Perfect Pecorino Romano Risotto (page 118) on my plate, blanket it with the grilled tomatoes and feta, and eat that combo for dinner. The resulting dish looks pretty and tastes amazing.

INGREDIENTS

2 tablespoons olive oil

3 large, ripe tomatoes, cored and sliced ¼-inch thick

¼ teaspoon dried oregano

¼ teaspoon dried basil

3 ounces crumbled feta cheese

Dash of freshly ground black pepper

Fresh basil, optional, for serving

DIRECTIONS

1. Preheat the grill on high.

2. Tear off a large sheet of aluminum foil and brush 1 tablespoon of the olive oil over it. Place the tomato slices on the greased foil. Sprinkle the oregano and basil over each slice and then drizzle the remaining olive oil over them.

3. Using a spoon or your fingers, distribute equal amounts of feta cheese on each tomato and then season with ground black pepper.

4. Lay the foil on the heated grill and close the grill. Allow the tomatoes to cook until the cheese has melted slightly and the tomatoes have released some of their juices, about 5 minutes. Arrange the tomato slices on a platter and surround with optional fresh basil leaves. Serve hot.

Satisfying Carrot-Ginger Slaw

SERVES 6 TO 8

The English word slaw is derived from the Dutch word for salad. In the United States we know it as a chilled, slightly soupy side of shredded cabbage, vinegar, and mayonnaise. In Satisfying Carrot-Ginger Slaw I keep the vinegar but change almost every other ingredient. The result is a moist yet crisp salad of juicy, shredded carrots, ginger, fennel, and a touch of lemon zest. It's a lighter and more refreshing take on coleslaw.

INGREDIENTS

2 pounds carrots, peeled

3 inches fresh ginger, peeled

1 small (roughly ½ pound) fennel bulb, trimmed

Zest of 1 lemon

3 tablespoons Champagne vinegar

1 tablespoon Dijon mustard

¼ cup extra virgin olive oil

½ teaspoon sea salt

¼ cup fresh minced cilantro

DIRECTIONS

1. Using a box or hand grater with wide holes, shred the carrots, ginger, and fennel into a large bowl. You want 1½- to 2-inch-long strips rather than small, slender chunks of each.

2. In a small bowl whisk together the zest, vinegar, mustard, olive oil, and salt. Pour the dressing over the slaw and toss to coat.

3. Refrigerate the slaw for at least 1 hour before serving. For best results, allow the ingredients to sit overnight.

4. Before serving, add the cilantro and toss to combine. Serve chilled.

Marvelous Parsnip Mash

SERVES 4 TO 6

Although they bear the shape and sweetness of carrots, parsnips have a spicy zing all their own. They jazz up stews and gratins but are also wonderful as a mash or puree. When mashed, their velveteen texture and spicy taste enhance a variety of mains including Soused Spinach and Tomato-Topped Mushrooms (page 56), Meatloaf Like Mom Should Have Made (page 80), Superb Steak Success Story (page 82), and Buttery Sea Scallops (page 66).

To make this parsnip mash a bit milder, creamier, and even more marvelous, I include a scant amount of potato.

INGREDIENTS

1½ pounds parsnips, peeled and chopped

10 ounces Russet potatoes, peeled and chopped

⅔ cup milk, at room temperature

3 tablespoons unsalted butter, melted

¼ teaspoon ground nutmeg

½ teaspoon salt, plus more as needed

¼ teaspoon ground white pepper, plus more as needed

Butter, optional, for serving

DIRECTIONS

1. Bring a large saucepan or small stockpot of water to a boil over medium-high heat. Add the parsnips and potatoes. Cook, uncovered, for 15 to 20 minutes, until the vegetables feel tender when probed with a fork.

2. Drain the vegetables and return them to the pan. Using either a potato ricer or masher, rice or mash the parsnips and potatoes in the pan. Stir together until combined.

3. Pour in the milk and melted butter. Stir until you have a smooth mash. Add the nutmeg, salt, and pepper and stir again. Taste and adjust the seasonings. Serve hot with an optional dollop of butter on top.

Get to Know Your Roots

As a kid, I ate a handful of root vegetables—beets, carrots, onions, and white and sweet potatoes. But there was a wealth of flavorful roots that I overlooked: the rose-and-white banded turnip, top-shaped rutabaga, tubular cassava or yucca root, bulbous jicama, petite radish, squat garlic, woody ginger, starchy yam, and, of course, that carrot-like parsnip. They all fall into the category of root vegetables.

Bursting with an abundance of vitamins and minerals, root vegetables are low in calories. Unfortunately, they also tend to be high in carbohydrates. Some low carb roots, such as radishes, onions, rutabagas, and turnips consist of over 90 percent water, making them both a moisture- and nutrient-rich addition to your cooking.

After washing and peeling your root veggies, you can boil, roast, bake, sauté, fry, braise, stew, or, in the case of radishes, carrots, onions, garlic, and ginger, serve raw.

Glistening Garlic-Pea Puree

SERVES 6 TO 8

Chances are that, even if you've never set foot on the British Isles, you have heard of the UK's fascination with fish, chips, and mushy peas. A lifelong loather of all pea varieties, I grudgingly tried a spoonful of these roughly mashed, tender, buttery peas at a London pub. That first bite made a pea lover out of me.

Glistening Garlic-Pea Puree is my tribute to that transformative dish and also to my childhood friends Marilee Morrow, Nickie Kolovos, and Ann Kerenyi. After years of enduring my love of all-things-British, these three joined me on a recent London trip and learned just how cool peas can be.

In the UK, cooks use marrowfat for mushy pea recipes. Larger than what we see in American markets, marrowfat peas are green peas left on the vine to mature and dry. Rather than special order these dried peas, I substitute frozen garden peas or English peas, which grocery stores commonly carry. Serve Glistening Garlic-Pea Puree hot alongside Soused Spinach and Tomato-Topped Mushrooms (page 56), Lavish Lime-Marinated Mackerel Kebabs (page 68), Superb Steak Success Story (page 82), or Meatloaf Like Mom Should Have Made (page 80). If you have any leftovers, eat them cold at lunchtime. That's how good these peas are.

INGREDIENTS

5 cups frozen peas

7 garlic cloves, peeled

3 tablespoons unsalted butter

¼ cup sour cream

¼ teaspoon ground white pepper

½ teaspoon sea salt

DIRECTIONS

1. Place the peas and garlic in a large saucepan filled with water. Bring the ingredients to a boil over medium-high heat. Once the ingredients are boiling, reduce the heat to medium. Allow the peas to cook until soft, 10 to 12 minutes. Remove the pan from the heat and drain.

2. Put the peas, garlic, and butter into the bowl of a food processor or blender and pulse to combine. Note that, depending on the size of your blender, you may need to make this in batches.

3. Scrape down the sides of the bowl with a spatula. Add the sour cream, pepper, and salt and pulse until the ingredients have a chunky but blended texture. Taste and adjust the seasonings if needed.

4. Spoon the pea puree into a large bowl and serve.

Smooth Goat Cheese Mashed Potatoes

SERVES 6

Mashed potatoes feel like velvet on your tongue. Soft, warm, and oh-so smooth, they remain one of the ultimate comfort foods. By including goat cheese, I bump up the creaminess of this classic and give it a more complex flavor.

Smooth Goat Cheese Mashed Potatoes pairs beautifully with most mains, including Lavish Lime-Marinated Mackerel Kebabs (page 68), Vegetarian or Meaty Sizzling Lentil-Stuffed Red Bell Peppers (page 59), and Velvety Poached Chicken with Tarragon-Shallot Sauce (page 77).

INGREDIENTS

2½ pounds Russet potatoes, peeled and quartered

4 ounces goat cheese, at room temperature

⅔ cup milk, warmed

4 tablespoons unsalted butter, at room temperature

Sea salt, to taste

Handful of fresh chives, diced

DIRECTIONS

1. Boil the potatoes in a large pot of salted water until tender, 10 to 12 minutes.

2. As the potatoes are cooking, whisk together the goat cheese and milk.

3. Drain the potatoes and either mash them by hand or push them through a potato ricer into the pot.

4. Using a heavy spatula or spoon, beat in the cheese mixture. Add the butter and salt, to taste, and stir to incorporate. Taste and add more salt, if needed.

5. Spoon the mashed potatoes into a serving bowl. Sprinkle the diced chives over the top. Serve hot.

Honeyed Sweet Potatoes

SERVES 4 TO 6

How can you not love sweet potatoes? They're sweet. They're luscious. Their cheery, orange color brightens any dinner table. Plus, they're rich in vitamin A and provide a good source of fiber, potassium, and other nutrients.

When selecting sweet potatoes, I seek out darker skinned, bruise-free tubers. Red or purple skin indicates that the sweet potato will have moist, sweet, soft, and orange or orange-red flesh. The white or yellow skinned varieties more resemble white potatoes and will be drier and less flavorful when cooked.

INGREDIENTS

3 pounds sweet potatoes

6 tablespoons unsalted butter

2 tablespoons honey

½ cup plus 1 tablespoon firmly packed light brown sugar

½ teaspoon ground cinnamon

¼ teaspoon ground nutmeg

Sea salt, to taste

DIRECTIONS

1. Leaving the skins on, boil the sweet potatoes in a large pot of lightly salted water until just tender, 15 to 20 minutes.

2. Remove the potatoes from the pan and allow them to cool slightly.

3. As the potatoes are cooling, melt the butter in a large frying or sauté pan over medium heat. Add the honey, sugar, cinnamon, and nutmeg and stir until well combined. Remove the pan from the heat.

4. Once the potatoes are cool enough to handle, remove and discard the skins. Slice the potatoes into chunks or half-moon slices and place them in the frying pan.

5. Over medium heat, toss together the potatoes and honeyed glaze until the potatoes are tender and have absorbed most of the glaze, about 5 minutes. Add salt, to taste.

6. Serve hot.

Which Is It, a Sweet Potato or a Yam?

Yams and sweet potatoes are not the same vegetable. Yet, people often confuse the two, referring to sweet potatoes as yams and advertising canned sweet potatoes as canned yams. Both are tropical root vegetables, but that is where the similarity ends.

In terms of looks, yams have rough, brown, bark-like skin and off-white to pinkish flesh. When cooked, they become starchy and develop a hint of sweetness. Popular in Latin American, Caribbean, African, and Asian cooking, yams are more difficult to find than sweet potatoes. I look for them at specialty grocery stores.

Unlike yams, sweet potatoes vary in skin color from yellow to red, and in flesh from yellow to deep orange. Smaller than yams, they resemble a medium-sized baking potato. When cooked, they possess a sweet flavor and moist texture. They are prevalent at markets in both fresh and canned forms.

LUSCIOUS, TENDER, JUICY

Exquisite European-Style Sautéed Mushrooms

SERVES 4

As a food writer who loves to travel, I've had the good fortune to cover Europe's festive, food-filled Christmas markets and sample an array of sweet and savory specialties. Among the memorable local dishes in which I've indulged, one of my favorites remains the sautéed mushrooms of Poland and Germany. Standing outdoors at makeshift, high-top tables on snowy nights, I shoveled in mouthful upon mouthful of steaming hot, earthy, seasoned mushrooms. Hearty and tasty, they warmed me to the core.

While I often ate sautéed mushrooms for dinner, today I serve them as a side for seafood and for such recipes as Lavish Lime-Marinated Mackerel Kebabs (page 68) and Meatloaf Like Mom Should Have Made (page 80). For a simple but filling entrée, mound them over slices of Danish brown or rye bread and serve. If you want to make this dish vegan-friendly, replace the butter with olive oil.

INGREDIENTS

3 tablespoons unsalted butter

¼ cup minced white onion

½ teaspoon salt

10 ounces white mushrooms, cleaned and halved

½ teaspoon paprika

¼ teaspoon granulated onion

¼ teaspoon garlic powder

2 tablespoons water, plus more as needed

DIRECTIONS

1. In a large frying pan melt half of the butter over medium heat. Add the onions and half of the salt and sauté for 2 to 3 minutes, until the onion has softened but is not browning.

2. Add the mushrooms, paprika, granulated onion, garlic powder, and 2 tablespoons water. Stirring periodically, cook until the mushrooms have softened and released some of their juices, about 10 minutes. If the pan and mushrooms become too dry, add more water. You want a small amount of sauce in the pan, but you do not want a soupy mixture.

3. Once the mushrooms have softened and browned slightly, remove the pan from the heat. Place the mushrooms in a large bowl or on individual plates. Serve warm as a side.

Savory Corn Custards

The word custard is derived from the French word croustade, and by definition custard is a blend of eggs and milk thickened by baking or simmering on the stove. In this form, without any additional ingredients, custard tastes exactly like what it is: eggs and milk cooked together. By including fruit, spices, cheese, vegetables, seafood, or meat, custard evolves into a dreamy, downright satisfying dish. Custard is the foundation for such sweets as crème brûlée and flan, and serves as the base for savory specialties such as Creamy Caramelized Onion Quiche (page 61) and this recipe.

To bake the Savory Corn Custards, you will use a water bath. For an explanation of water baths or bain-maries, flip to the recipe for Sultry Caribbean Jerk Chicken (page 74).

INGREDIENTS

2 tablespoons unsalted butter

3 cups fresh or frozen corn

2 garlic cloves, minced

2 large eggs

1½ cups milk

1 teaspoon sea salt

¼ teaspoon ground black pepper

DIRECTIONS

1. Preheat the oven to 350°F. Grease four 5-ounce ramekins or ovenproof bowls.

2. Melt the butter in a medium sauté pan. Add the corn and garlic and sauté until softened, 3 to 5 minutes. Remove the corn from the heat and allow it to cool slightly.

3. Place half of the corn in the bowl of a food processor or blender. Pulse until pureed.

4. In a large bowl or pitcher whisk together the eggs, milk, salt, and pepper. Add the sautéed and pureed corn to the bowl and whisk to combine.

5. Pour the custard mixture into the greased ramekins. Place the ramekins in a baking pan filled with enough warm water to reach halfway up their sides.

6. Bake for 50 to 60 minutes, until the custards have puffed up and browned slightly. Serve hot.

Zesty Zucchini and Tomato Gratin

SERVES 6

In spite of its rather fancy sounding French name, a gratin is simply a baked dish with a crisp top crust made from bread crumbs and/or cheese. Here the crunchy topping provides a nice contrast to the silken vegetables.

This gratin goes well with Lavish Lime-Marinated Mackerel Kebabs (page 68), Meatloaf like Mom Should Have Made (page 80), and Superb Steak Success Story (page 82). Gratins usually act as sides, but when this gratin is paired with another filling side such as Saucy Italian Bread Salad (page 94), Smooth Goat Cheese Mashed Potatoes (page 109), or Perfect Pecorino Romano Risotto (page 118), you can make it a scrumptious meal.

INGREDIENTS

2 tablespoons olive oil

2 zucchinis, sliced into ¼-inch-thick rounds

1 teaspoon salt

1 small Spanish onion, chopped

1 garlic clove, minced

1 teaspoon dried marjoram

½ teaspoon red pepper flakes

2 large ripe tomatoes, cored and cut into ¼-inch-thick slices

Ground white pepper, to taste

1 cup Panko bread crumbs

½ cup grated Pecorino Romano cheese

1½ tablespoons extra virgin olive oil

DIRECTIONS

1. Preheat the oven to 450°F. Grease the bottom and sides of 10-by-8-inch or similarly sized baking dish with 1 tablespoon olive oil.

2. Place the zucchini rounds on clean towels or paper towels. Sprinkle half of the salt over the zucchini and allow it to sit for 15 minutes.

3. Heat the other tablespoon of olive oil in a small frying pan over medium heat. Add the onion, garlic, and remaining salt.

4. Sauté until the onions and garlic have softened and begin to turn translucent, 3 to 5 minutes. Add the marjoram and red pepper flakes and stir to combine. Remove the pan from the heat and set aside.

5. With a clean towel blot the zucchini slices to remove any excess liquid and salt.

6. Evenly spread half of the zucchini in a layer on the bottom of the baking dish. Cover the zucchini with half of the cooked onions and then overlap half of the tomato slices on top of them. Repeat with the remaining zucchini, onions, and tomato. Sprinkle the white pepper over the top layer of the tomatoes.

7. Toss together the bread crumbs, cheese, and extra virgin olive oil. Scatter the topping over the tomatoes.

8. Bake, uncovered, for 15 minutes or until the topping has turned golden and the tomatoes have softened. Serve warm.

Perfect Pecorino Romano Risotto

SERVES 6 TO 8 AS A SIDE OR 4 AS AN ENTREE

The first time I set out to make risotto, I thought, "All that effort for a bowl of rice?" Then I tasted my concoction and realized that, yes, that bowl of rice was worth the time and effort. Risotto needs time to plump up with delicious, warm stock. It needs time to soften and become lush. It needs time to develop into the lavish specialty that it is.

Perfect Pecorino Romano Risotto goes well with a long list of main dishes, including Soused Spinach and Tomato-Topped Mushrooms (page 56), Luscious Lemon-Garlic Shrimp (page 64), Lavish Lime-Marinated Mackerel Kebabs (page 68), and Superb Steak Success Story (page 82). I find it filling enough to eat on its own for dinner. I have also served it with another side such as asparagus, Zesty Zucchini and Tomato Gratin (page 117) or Exquisite European-Style Sautéed Mushrooms (page 113).

INGREDIENTS

4½ cups chicken stock

½ cup dry white wine

2 tablespoons unsalted butter

1 small white onion, pureed in a food processor or blender

1½ cups Arborio rice

3 ounces grated Pecorino Romano cheese

1 teaspoon sea salt

¼ teaspoon ground white pepper

DIRECTIONS

1. Heat the stock and white wine in a large saucepan over medium heat.

2. Melt the butter in another large saucepan over medium heat. Add the onions to the pan and cook, stirring occasionally, until soft and translucent, 5 to 7 minutes.

3. Stir in the rice, making sure that the rice is coated with the buttery onions. Cook until the rice releases a toasted aroma, about 1 minute.

4. Using a ladle or measuring cup, add roughly a third of the heated liquid to the rice. Stirring constantly, cook the rice until it absorbs almost all the liquid. At this point add another third of the liquid and, continually stirring, cook until the liquid is absorbed. Repeat until the rice is soft and creamy and the liquid is gone, about 25 minutes total.

5. Sprinkle in the cheese, salt, and pepper. Stir until well combined. Serve hot.

Sensational South Indian Ven Pongal

SERVES 4

In South India, this tender, aromatic dish is served at breakfast. Because it's so robust and flavorful, I have added it to my evening menus. Its nutty, mildly garlic flavor pairs nicely with fish and shellfish, including Buttery Sea Scallops (page 66).

With the exception of ghee and asafoetida powder, you should be able to find the following ingredients at your local supermarket. If you can't locate ghee, substitute clarified butter. As for asafoetida, it can be found in Asian markets. If you don't have an Asian market near you, replace the asafoetida with garlic powder. Asafoetida appears frequently in Indian recipes and is derived from fennel. It adds a mellow, garlic flavor to foods. If you do go with garlic powder, increase the amount in the recipe to ¼ teaspoon.

INGREDIENTS

⅓ cup moong dal

½ cup plus 2 tablespoons white rice

1 teaspoon cumin seeds, toasted

3½ cups water

⅛ teaspoon asafoetida powder

⅛ teaspoon ground ginger

1 teaspoon sea salt

1 tablespoon olive oil

2 tablespoons ghee or clarified butter

1 teaspoon black peppercorns, crushed lightly with the back of a spoon

12 to 14 whole cashews

DIRECTIONS

1. In a small frying pan over medium heat, toast the moong dal until it releases its aroma, 2 to 3 minutes. Remove the pan from the heat.

2. Place the dal and rice in a colander. Rinse them under cold running water and drain.

3. Toast the cumin seeds in a small frying pan over medium heat until they release their aroma, about 1 minute. Remove the pan from heat.

4. Place half of the seeds in a large, heavy bottomed pan. Add the rice, dal, water, asafoetida, ginger, and salt to the pan and bring the ingredients to a boil over high heat.

5. Once the water has begun to boil, put a tight fitting lid on the pot and reduce the heat to medium. Simmer the ingredients for 16 to 20 minutes, until all the water has been absorbed and the rice and dal are very soft. Remove the pan from the heat and, leaving the lid on, set it aside.

6. Heat the olive oil and ghee in a large frying pan over medium heat. Add the remaining cumin seeds, peppercorns, and cashews and cook for 1 minute.

7. Using a spoon or spatula, mash the rice and dal together until smooth. Add the mixture to the frying pan and stir together until well combined. Serve warm.

Luxurious Cakes, Pies, and Puddings

DESSERT LOVERS UNITE! IT IS TIME TO talk about some of the most toothsome treats in the land of sweets, cakes, pies, and puddings. Just imagine a velvety iced cake, glittering fruit tart, or saucy baked pudding—desserts so luscious and dreamy, they practically slide off their plates!

Cakes come in a wide range of types, including sponge, nut, fruit, and ice cream. They also have a variety of shapes, such as the rectangular sheet, round layer, jelly roll, Bundt, loaf, and more. No matter the shape, a cake's ingredients and mixing and baking techniques will determine how moist and tender it is.

Regarding mixing methods, the following cake recipes use straight-mix, creaming, or foaming. With straight-mix, you sift the dry ingredients (flour, salt, baking powder, and/or baking soda) into one bowl and put the wet ingredients (melted butter or oil, eggs, and any other liquids) in another. Whisk each group separately before blending them together for a luxurious cake. Aunt Nancy's Stupendous Carrot Cake (page 1134) employs the straight-mix method.

With the creaming method you begin by beating together butter and sugar until the two are light and creamy. You then add eggs, one at a time, beating until all the ingredients are incorporated. Finally, you stir in the flour and any other dry ingredients. Ambrosial Apricot Upside-Down Cake (page 127) and Double Apple-Spice Cake (page 136) use the creaming method.

Foaming, or whisking as it's sometimes called, requires you to beat whole eggs, egg whites, or yolks until they're light and frothy. Once you have achieved this texture, you fold sugar, flour, and any other ingredients into the foam to create a soft, airy cake. Everyone Loves Lamingtons (page 130), My Favorite Victoria Sponge (page 132), and Fabulous and Flourless White Chocolate-Almond Torte (page 139) feature foaming.

Scrumptious desserts don't start and end with cake. We have pies, too! Although not quite as vast with their shapes and types, pies offer a wealth of flavors and moist fillings. In the following pages we'll cover two of the most common pies, fruit and nut, in Molten Mince Pie (page 147), To-Die-for Tarte Tatin (page 140), and Ethereal Pear-Frangipane Tart (page 140).

You might wonder what distinguishes a pie from a tart. It comes down to crust. Pies generally have both a bottom and top crust composed of flour, butter or lard, water, and salt. Tarts, on the other hand, possess only a bottom crust made from rich, crumbly pâtée brisée or egg- and sugar-laced pâté sucrée.

From pies we move on to puddings. These are not the familiar milky, rice- or tapioca-studded confections. Nor are they thick, creamy, cornstarch-based treats. Instead, these satisfying sweets contain flour, cookies, or custard. Baked in individual cups or a baking dish, the resulting puddings resemble extremely moist cakes. When served with a sauce, as Sticky Toffee Puddings (page 151), these desserts dazzle with their dulcet consistency.

A quick note about the term *pudding*. While Americans tend to think of pudding as either a creamy or breadlike sweet, residents of the United Kingdom and former British Commonwealth nations refer to all desserts as pudding. If you visit the UK, Ireland, Australia, New Zealand, or other Commonwealths and are offered a pudding at the end of your meal, don't be shocked when your host serves you a slice of cake or tart.

Heavenly Honey Cake

SERVES 8 TO 10

Recipes for honey-sweetened cakes have existed for centuries. In ancient times Egyptians, Greeks, and Romans presented honey cakes as offerings to their gods. Today, bakers around the globe offer these moist confections at festive gatherings, religious holidays, and New Year's festivities. Honey cakes are said to promote good luck or sweetness in the days and weeks to come. My motivation for baking a Heavenly Honey Cake is much simpler. I just like satiny, fragrant, and richly flavored cakes, and Heavenly Honey Cake fits that description.

To make your cake even more heavenly, prick holes into the top before drizzling the honey over it. The honey will ooze down into the cake, transforming it into an extremely damp and delicious sweet.

INGREDIENTS

FOR THE CAKE

1¾ cups all-purpose flour

¾ teaspoon baking powder

½ teaspoon baking soda

1 teaspoon salt

1 teaspoon ground cinnamon

¼ teaspoon ground nutmeg

2 large eggs

½ cup firmly packed light brown sugar

¼ cup granulated sugar

⅔ cup honey

½ cup milk

½ cup olive oil

1 teaspoon vanilla extract

½ teaspoon lemon juice

FOR THE ALMOND TOPPING

⅔ cup sliced blanched almonds

3 to 4 tablespoons confectioners' sugar

FOR THE HONEY SYRUP

½ cup honey

1 teaspoon water

(Continued)

DIRECTIONS

1. Preheat the oven to 350°F. Grease and dust with flour a 9-inch springform pan.

2. In a large bowl combine the flour, baking powder, baking soda, salt, cinnamon, and nutmeg.

3. In a separate bowl using either a stand or hand mixer, beat together the eggs and two sugars until thick and pale brown, about 3 minutes. Scrape down the sides of the bowl.

4. In another bowl, whisk together the honey, milk, oil, vanilla, and lemon juice. Beat this into egg mixture and scrape down the sides of the mixing bowl.

5. Add half of the flour mixture and beat on low speed. Scrape down the sides of the bowl, add the remaining flour and beat until combined.

6. Pour the batter into the prepared pan. Bake until golden and a cake tester inserted in the center comes out clean, about 45 minutes. Remove the cake from the oven and allow it to cool on a wire rack for 15 minutes.

7. While the cake is cooling, make your almond topping. Place the sliced almonds in a frying pan and toast, stirring occasionally, over medium-low heat until the nuts glisten, become golden in color, and release their aroma, 2 to 3 minutes.

8. Add half of the confectioners' sugar to the pan and stir until the nuts are coated. Remove the pan from the heat and put the nuts in a heatproof bowl.

9. To loosen the cake from the pan, run a sharp, thin-bladed knife around its edges. Unlock the springform pan, remove the cake, and place it on a cake plate or stand. Prick holes in the top of the cake with a fork.

10. Warm the honey and water in a small pan over medium heat for 30 seconds to 1 minute. Pour the syrup over the cake.

11. Spread the candied almonds over the top and dust with the remaining confectioners' sugar. Let the cake sit for an hour to soak up the syrup.

12. Slice and serve with tea or coffee.

Ambrosial Apricot Upside-Down Cake

SERVES 8

Traditionally, upside-down cake features canned pineapple rings. In fact, the dessert was created to encourage the use of this tinned fruit. Because I adore the silken texture and honeyed flavor of apricots, I replace the usual pineapple rings with sliced apricots for an Ambrosial Apricot Upside-Down Cake. You can also substitute fresh or canned peaches in this recipe.

To give this cake a more luscious texture, I use buttermilk instead of whole milk in the batter. Although lower in fat than whole milk, buttermilk's thick consistency gives the batter a richer texture. Slightly acidic in nature, it impairs the formation of gluten, which, in turn, makes the cake tenderer.

INGREDIENTS

FOR THE TOPPING

4 tablespoons unsalted butter, melted

⅔ cup firmly packed light brown sugar

6 to 8 fresh or canned apricots, peeled and cut into ½-inch-thick slices

FOR THE CAKE

1¼ cups all-purpose flour

½ teaspoon baking powder

¼ teaspoon baking soda

¼ teaspoon salt

5 tablespoons unsalted butter, at room temperature

¾ cup granulated sugar

2 large eggs, at room temperature

1 teaspoon vanilla extract

⅔ cup buttermilk, at room temperature

Whipped cream, optional, for serving

DIRECTIONS

1. Preheat the oven to 350°F.

2. Pour the melted butter into a 9-inch cast-iron skillet or 9-by-2-inch round pan. Swirl the butter in the bottom of the pan until it is evenly coated.

3. Spread the brown sugar over the butter. Place the apricots, cut sides up, on top of the sugar. You should have one layer of apricots, just touching each other.

4. For the cake, in a large bowl sift together the flour, baking powder, baking soda, and salt. Set the bowl aside.

(Continued)

5. In another large bowl, using an electric stand or hand mixer, beat together the softened butter and sugar until light and creamy, 2 to 3 minutes. Scrape down the sides of the bowl and add the eggs and vanilla. Beat until fluffy, 1 to 2 minutes.

6. After scraping down the sides of the bowl again, add a third of the flour and mix on low to combine. Scrape down the sides of the bowl and add half of the buttermilk, mixing on low. Repeat until all the flour and buttermilk have been incorporated into the batter.

7. Spoon the batter into the skillet or pan, spreading it evenly over the fruit and sugar.

8. Bake for 35 to 45 minutes, until the cake is golden in color and a toothpick inserted in the cake's center comes out clean.

9. Remove the pan from the oven and place on a wire rack to cool for 5 minutes.

10. Invert a large serving platter over the cake. Using oven mitts, and with the platter pressed against the cake, carefully lift and invert the cake pan onto the platter. The cake will now be upside down on the platter. Gently lift up the pan. If any fruit or sugary syrup remains in the pan, remove and evenly spread it over the cake. Serve warm or at room temperature with an optional dollop of whipped cream on top.

Picking the Right Baking Pan

Some baking recipes call for round or layer cake pans. Others want you to use springform pans. Here are the differences between the two and why you shouldn't make an upside-down cake in a springform pan.

Fashioned from a single piece of metal and featuring a rolled rim at the top, a round or layer cake pan is perfect for layer cakes or extremely dense, wet cakes. The pan heats and bakes evenly and creates a uniformly shaped cake. Because the pan has no seams or openings, it's ideal for a wet-bottomed upside-down cake. None of the cake's honeyed topping will leak out of this pan.

Consisting of a removable metal bottom and sides, a springform pan is used for delicate cakes, including sponges and tortes. To remove the cake, you flick open a side clamp and gently lift off the sides, leaving the cake and base behind. If you want to remove the base, allow the cake to cool slightly before gently inverting the cake onto a plate or wire rack and lifting off the bottom. With a springform pan your fragile cake will remain in one piece. Due to the seams and removable parts, a springform pan is not a good choice for an upside-down cake. In all likelihood the cake's luscious topping will ooze out through the seam around the bottom.

Everyone Loves Lamingtons

MAKES TWELVE 2-INCH SQUARES

This delightful, individual-sized, Australian treat features moist sponge cake. Sponge cake gets its name, in part, from the tiny air bubbles trapped in the batter. It also comes from the cake's ability to soak up liquids as a sponge would. This consistency results from the high proportion of eggs to flour and the use of the foaming method of mixing. This form of mixing is discussed in the opening section of this chapter.

INGREDIENTS

FOR THE SPONGE

7 large eggs, at room temperature, yolks and whites separated

1⅓ cups granulated sugar

1½ teaspoons vanilla extract

1 cup all-purpose flour, sifted

FOR THE FILLING

½ cup plus 1 tablespoon good-quality strawberry or raspberry jam

FOR THE TOPPING

1 pound confectioners' sugar

1 cup unsweetened cocoa powder

1 teaspoon vanilla extract

¾ cup water

3 cups shredded, sweetened coconut

DIRECTIONS

1. Preheat the oven to 350°F. Line the bottom of a 9-inch springform pan with parchment paper.

2. For the sponge, in a medium bowl, beat together the egg yolks, 1 cup of the sugar, and vanilla extract until light in color and fluffy, 3 to 4 minutes.

3. In a separate bowl beat the egg whites until soft peaks form. Add the remaining $^1/_3$ cup sugar and beat until stiff, glossy peaks form.

4. Using a spatula, gently fold a third of the egg whites into the egg yolk mixture. Once the egg whites have been incorporated, fold in a third of the sifted flour. Repeat until you have a soft, fluffy batter.

5. Spoon the batter into the springform pan. Place the pan in the oven and lower the temperature to 325°F.

6. Bake for 25 to 30 minutes, until golden in color and a toothpick or cake tester inserted in the center of the cake comes out clean.

7. To cool, invert the cake on a wire cooling rack. After an hour remove the cake from the pan. You may need to use a thin, sharp knife to separate the cake from the pan before attempting to remove it. Cool completely before slicing.

8. Using a thin-bladed, sharp knife, slice the cake in half horizontally. Remove the top half and set aside. Spread the jam evenly over the other half, coating the entire top surface. Place the top half back onto the cake.

9. With a serrated knife, trim the edges on the cake so that you have a square shape. Slice the cake into 12 squares.

10. For the topping, in a medium bowl, whisk together the confectioners' sugar, cocoa powder, vanilla extract, and water. Place the shredded coconut in a separate bowl.

11. Using a fork or tongs, dip a cake square into the chocolate glaze. Allow any extra glaze to drip off before dunking the cake into the coconut and covering all sides with it. Place the finished Lamington onto a sheet of parchment paper and allow the glaze to set. Repeat until all the Lamingtons have been made.

Tips for a Soft, Airy Sponge Cake

What differentiates a sponge from other cakes is the high proportion of eggs to flour. In this recipe for lamingtons, the ratio is not quite two eggs to ¼ cup of flour. This excess of eggs results in the airy, springy consistency for which sponge cake is known. How you work with these eggs is important. You should bring the eggs to room temperature before using them. Room temperature eggs whip more easily and hold more air than cold eggs. Remember to beat the egg yolks until they're pale, fluffy, and filled with air. This also increases the cake's lightness.

To add even more air, sift the flour for the batter. Gently fold the sifted flour into the wet ingredients. Be careful not to overmix them.

Some sponge recipes omit butter and oil. This omission will make the sponge lighter. However, when butter is part of the recipe, as is the case in My Favorite Victoria Sponge, it should be room temperature but not mushy. Squishy butter produces a dense instead of airy cake. Cold, hard butter leads to overmixing, which also yields a heavy cake.

My Favorite Victoria Sponge

SERVES 8

Victoria sponge is named for England's Queen Victoria, who apparently loved a slice of this sweet with her afternoon tea. Shortly after her reign, this cake became a staple at early 20th century British parties and teas. I first tried this heavenly cake at a teashop in England's Lake District. Sweet yet airy, it surpassed all my expectations. Serve with a cup of hot, black tea.

If you struggle with horizontally halving a cake, you can divide the batter between two greased, 7-inch springform pans. The slender cakes will bake for 12 to 15 minutes; this is slightly less than what's required for an 8-inch pan. The jam and icing will then be spread between the two cooled cakes instead of between a halved cake.

INGREDIENTS

FOR THE SPONGE

1 stick (8 tablespoons) unsalted butter, at room temperature

⅔ cup granulated sugar

3 large eggs, at room temperature

1 teaspoon vanilla extract

1 tablespoon milk, at room temperature

1 cup all-purpose flour

1½ teaspoons baking powder

Pinch of salt

FOR THE ICING

1 stick (8 tablespoons) unsalted butter, at room temperature

1 teaspoon vanilla extract

¼ cup milk, at room temperature

1 pound confectioners' sugar

⅔ cup good-quality strawberry jam

DIRECTIONS

1. Preheat the oven to 375°F. Grease one 8-inch springform pan and set aside.

2. For the sponge, in a large mixing bowl beat the butter until creamy, 2 minutes. Scrape down the sides, add the sugar and beat again until light and fluffy, 5 minutes. Scrape down the bowl again, add the eggs, vanilla, and milk and beat until combined.

3. Sift together the flour, baking powder, and salt. Add the flour mixture and gently fold it into the liquids.

4. Place the batter in the greased pan. Bake for 16 to 20 minutes, until the cake has risen and is golden in color. Remove the cake from the oven and cool for 10 minutes before removing it from the pan and cooling completely on a wire rack.

5. To make the icing, in a large mixing bowl beat the butter, vanilla, and milk together until smooth. With the mixer running on low, slowly add the confectioners' sugar, beating until creamy and smooth.

6. Using a long, sharp, serrated knife, cut the cake, widthwise, into two equal-sized halves. Put one half, cut side up, on a platter. Spread half of the icing, followed by all the jam, on the cut side. Lay the other half of the cake, cut side down, on top of this layer.

7. Spread the remaining icing over the top of it.

What Folding Does for a Batter

When you fold ingredients in a bowl, you are gently mixing them together by hand. Using a rubber spatula, you carefully scoop up and turn over the ingredients until they are combined. By folding you ensure that air bubbles are not released from the batter. These bubbles help to create and maintain an airy texture.

Folding enables us to combine light and dense mixtures. An example of this would be folding whipped egg whites into the nutty batter in Fabulous and Flourless White Chocolate-Almond Torte. The resulting folded batter is light and supple. Sponge cakes, tortes, and other delicate baked goods call for this method of mixing.

Aunt Nancy's Stupendous Carrot Cake

SERVES 10 TO 12

We should all be so lucky to have an Aunt Nancy, a woman who selflessly shares the secret recipe for her insanely velvety carrot cake. I have my husband to thank for bringing his Aunt Nancy Haberberger into my life, and I've been baking a version of her carrot cake for so long that I sometimes forget she wasn't the creator of this sweet. Depending upon whom you consult, it was the British, the French, or the Swiss who invented the moist, aromatic, carrot-laced treat.

To plump up the raisins in this cake, I place them in a pan with enough water to cover them. I then simmer them over medium heat for 5 minutes. After taking the pan off the burner, I allow the raisins to sit for 10 minutes. From there I drain, towel dry, and add them to the cake batter. If you prefer chewy raisins, feel free to ignore this step.

INGREDIENTS

FOR THE CAKE

1 cup firmly packed light brown sugar

1 cup granulated sugar

1½ cups vegetable oil

4 large eggs

2 cups all-purpose flour

2 teaspoons baking soda

2 teaspoons ground cinnamon

1 teaspoon salt

3 cups grated carrots

1 cup roughly chopped walnuts

1 cup raisins

FOR THE ICING

1 stick unsalted butter, softened

8 ounces cream cheese

1 teaspoon vanilla extract

1 pound confectioners' sugar, sifted

DIRECTIONS

1. Preheat the oven to 325°F. Grease and flour a 9-by-13-inch baking pan or two 9-inch layer or springform pans. If using springform pans, line the bottom of the pans with parchment paper before greasing and flouring.

2. Using an electric mixer, in a large bowl beat together the sugars, oil, and eggs.

3. In a separate bowl sift together the flour, baking soda, cinnamon, and salt. Add the dry ingredients to the liquids, beating on low speed until incorporated and then beating on high until well blended. Scrape down the sides of the bowl and then add the carrots, nuts, and raisins. Mix the ingredients together either on low speed or by hand until combined.

4. Pour the batter into the prepared pan(s). Bake for 50 to 60 minutes, until a toothpick inserted in the center comes out clean. Place the cake pan(s) on a wire rack to cool. If using springform pans, after 10 minutes remove the cakes from the pans, invert them onto cooling racks and peel the parchment paper from their bottoms. Cool completely before icing.

5. To make the icing, place the butter and cream cheese in a large bowl. Using an electric hand or stand mixer, beat until the two are smooth and creamy, about 5 minutes. Add the vanilla and beat again to combine. Slowly add the confectioners' sugar, mixing on low speed until incorporated and then beating on high speed until blended.

6. Using a knife or icing spatula, spread the icing evenly over the cake(s). Slice and serve.

Double Apple-Spice Cake

SERVES 8 TO 10

This soft, aromatic, apple-studded cake lends itself quite nicely to breakfast time. If you want to bake and serve this as a morning treat, consider leaving off the glaze. Although I love the white, sugary topping, it does make the cake sweeter and a bit less wholesome for breakfast.

INGREDIENTS

FOR THE CAKE

1 stick (8 tablespoons) unsalted butter, at room temperature

1 cup firmly packed light brown sugar

1 large egg, at room temperature

2 tablespoons plus 1 teaspoon honey

1½ cups all-purpose flour

1 teaspoon baking soda

½ teaspoon salt

1 teaspoon ground cinnamon

½ teaspoon ground cardamom

⅛ teaspoon ground nutmeg

1 cup unsweetened applesauce

2 Granny Smith apples, peeled and chopped

FOR THE GLAZE

3 tablespoons water

1 teaspoon vanilla extract

1½ cups confectioners' sugar

DIRECTIONS

1. Preheat the oven to 350°F. Line the bottom of an 8-inch round pan with parchment paper. Grease and then flour the pan and parchment paper.

2. Using an electric stand or hand mixer, beat the butter until creamy, about 1 minute. Add the brown sugar and beat again until creamy, 2 to 3 minutes. Scrape down the sides of the bowl. Add the egg and honey and beat until combined.

3. In a separate bowl, whisk together the flour, baking soda, salt, cinnamon, cardamom, and nutmeg.

4. Add the dry ingredients to the wet, beating together until combined. Scrape down the sides of the mixing bowl. Add the applesauce and beat again. Scrape down the bowl and stir in the chopped apples.

5. Spoon the batter into the prepared cake pan and smooth out the top. You want the batter to be evenly distributed.

6. Bake for 50 minutes or until the cake appears firm and a cake tester or toothpick inserted into the center comes out clean. Note that after 35 minutes you may need to cover the top with foil so that the cake doesn't brown too much.

7. Cool for 5 minutes on a wire rack before removing the cake from the pan and allowing it to cool completely. After it has cooled, make the glaze for the cake.

8. To make the glaze, whisk together the water, vanilla, and confectioners' sugar. Pour it over the top of the cake. Allow it to set before serving.

So Many Apples. Which One to Choose?

With thousands of apple varieties in existence around the world and over a dozen varieties sold in United States markets, it can be tough to choose the right apple for baking or cooking. I won't even get into the right apple for eating. That pertains more to personal taste and availability.

For baking, you should select firm, sweetly tart apples that keep their shape and don't get mushy when exposed to high temperatures. Granny Smith, Jonagold, Cortland, Braeburn, and Honeycrisp all fit the criteria. When shopping for apples, choose firm, unblemished, young fruit. Although apples will keep for several weeks unrefrigerated, for the best results use them shortly after purchasing.

Fabulous and Flourless
White Chocolate-Almond Torte

SERVES 8 TO 10

When I bake this torte in late fall and winter, I top it with pomegranate seeds or chunky, homemade cranberry sauce. In spring, summer, and early fall I dress it with a mix of seasonal berries such as strawberries, raspberries, blueberries, and blackberries. One of my go-to desserts, Fabulous and Flourless White Chocolate-Almond Torte is perfect for gluten-free guests as well as anyone who enjoys a lush cake.

INGREDIENTS

1½ cups blanched almonds

10 tablespoons unsalted butter, at room temperature

⅓ cup granulated sugar

6 large eggs, separated

7 ounces (1 cup plus 1½ teaspoons) white chocolate morsels, melted and cooled

2 teaspoons almond extract

Confectioners' sugar, for dusting

4 cups mixed seasonal berries

DIRECTIONS

1. Preheat the oven to 350°F. Line the bottom of a 9-inch springform pan with parchment paper and then grease the pan and paper. Set aside.

2. Put the blanched almonds in the bowl of a food processor or blender and pulse until ground. Set aside.

3. Using an electric mixer, beat the butter until smooth and light in color, 2 to 3 minutes.

Scrape down the sides of the bowl and add half of the sugar. Continue beating until fluffy, 1 to 2 minutes. Scrape down the sides of the bowl and then add the egg yolks one at a time, beating and scraping down the bowl after each addition.

4. Spoon in the cooled, melted chocolate and beat until well combined. At this point add the ground almonds and almond extract and beat until incorporated.

5. In a separate bowl and using an electric mixer, beat the egg whites until soft peaks form. Add the remaining sugar. Continue beating until stiff, glossy peaks form.

6. Using a rubber spatula, fold the egg whites into the nutty batter. Don't overmix; you want the batter to be airy yet chunky. Evenly spread the mixture in the springform pan.

7. Bake for 45 to 50 minutes, until the cake starts to separate from the sides of the pan. Remove the cake from the oven and allow it to cool in the pan for 15 minutes.

8. Gently run a thin-bladed knife around the edge of the cake, separating it completely from the pan. Unlock and remove the sides of the springform pan. Using the same knife, loosen the cake from the bottom of the pan and remove the parchment round. Place the cake on a wire rack to cool completely.

9. Before serving, dust the top of the cake with confectioners' sugar. Spread the fruit over the sugar and then dust again.

To-Die-for Tarte Tatin

SERVES 6

An early 20th-century France creation, and named for the Tatin sisters who popularized it in their restaurant, tarte tatin sounds rather fancy. In reality it's a quick, rustic apple tart that's baked upside down and served right side up.

To-Die-for Tarte Tatin gets its lush texture from the apple juices and caramelized sugar that saturate the buttery puff pastry. It is at its tender best when consumed the same day that it's made.

INGREDIENTS

5 tablespoons unsalted butter

¾ cup granulated sugar

¼ teaspoon ground cinnamon

⅛ teaspoon ground nutmeg

Pinch of ground ginger

6 Granny Smith or other tart apples, peeled, cored, and sliced

1 sheet puff pastry, homemade (page 22) or store-bought

Whipped cream, optional, for serving

Ice cream, optional, for serving

DIRECTIONS

1. Preheat the oven to 375°F.

2. Melt the butter in a 9-inch, oven-safe frying pan over medium heat. Stir in the sugar, cinnamon, nutmeg, and ginger.

3. Place the apples, cut side down, in the pan and cook over medium heat until a light colored caramel forms, about 10 minutes.

4. Place the puff pastry over the apples and tuck in the pastry edges. Poke a few holes in the top of the pastry.

5. Place the tart in the preheated oven and bake for 20 minutes or until the pastry is golden and puffed up. Remove the pan from the oven and place it on a cooling rack for 10 minutes.

6. Lay a large, round plate face down over the frying pan. Holding the plate firmly over the tart with one hand and the pan's handle with the other, turn over the pan and invert the tart onto the plate. Don't worry if the syrup oozes over the plate. That's supposed to happen.

7. Slice the tart and serve warm with an optional topping of whipped cream and/or ice cream.

Ethereal Pear-Frangipane Tart

SERVES 8

This tart gets its wondrous texture from multiple sources—the silky crust, succulent pears, and alluring almond filling known as frangipane. You will find frangipane in such desserts as galette des rois, or king cake, and Bakewell tarts. Although, like marzipan, frangipane is made from almonds, it is not the same as marzipan. Frangipane has a creamy, pliable texture while marzipan has a firmer, candylike consistency similar to fondant.

If you don't have time to make a homemade piecrust, feel free to use a store-bought sweet tart crust. Likewise, if you're not a fan of pears, feel free to replace that fruit with plums, peaches, or nectarines. The tart will be just as moist and delicious.

INGREDIENTS

FOR THE CRUST

1⅓ cups all-purpose flour

Pinch of salt

¼ cup granulated sugar

6 tablespoons cold unsalted butter, cut into small chunks

1 tablespoon olive oil

1 tablespoon heavy cream

1 large egg yolk

FOR THE FRANGIPANE

1 stick (8 tablespoons) unsalted butter, at room temperature

¾ cup plus 2 tablespoons granulated sugar

1 large egg, at room temperature

1 large egg yolk, at room temperature

1 teaspoon almond extract

7 ounces ground, blanched almonds or almond meal

3 tablespoons cake flour

FOR THE TART

Frangipane

Tart crust

6 canned or poached pear halves, drained

⅓ cup sliced almonds

Confectioners' sugar, to dust the top of the tart

DIRECTIONS

1. To make the tart crust, stir together the flour, salt, and sugar in a large bowl. Using a fork or pastry cutter, cut the butter into the flour until a crumbly mixture forms. Stir in the olive oil, cream, and egg yolk.

2. Using your hands, knead the dough until it becomes soft and fairly smooth in texture, 1 to 2 minutes.

3. Shape the dough into a ball and place it on a lightly floured work surface. Using a lightly dusted rolling pin, roll out the dough until it

(Continued)

is about 11 inches in diameter. Gently lower the dough into a 10-inch tart pan and pat into place. Slice off and discard any extra dough hanging over the edge of the pan. Refrigerate the crust for at least 30 minutes.

4. Preheat the oven to 400°F.

5. After placing pie weights or dried beans in your tart pan, bake the crust for 10 minutes. Reduce the heat to 375°F, remove the weights and bake for another 10 minutes, until golden in color. Leaving the oven on, remove the tart pan and set aside.

6. To make the frangipane, you will need an electric stand or hand mixer. In a large bowl beat together the butter and sugar until light and creamy, 2 to 3 minutes. Scrape down the sides of the bowl and add the egg, egg yolk, and almond extract. Beat to combine and then scrape down the sides of the bowl again.

7. Add the blanched almonds and cake flour. Mix on low speed until incorporated, less than 1 minute.

8. To assemble the tart, evenly spread the frangipane over the crust. Place the halved pears on top of the frangipane, in a concentric circle, with the cut sides down. Bake the tart for 25 minutes.

9. Remove the tart from the oven and sprinkle the sliced almonds over it. Return the tart to the oven and bake for another 8 to 10 minutes, until the crust and almonds are golden brown.

10. Completely cool the tart on a wire rack. Before serving, dust the top with confectioners' sugar.

Scrumptious Sweet Potato Pie

SERVES 8

Sweet potato pie is a specialty of the American South, where it is rumored to be in every regional cookbook. No wonder! Possessing a sweet, lightly spiced flavor and intoxicating aroma, this pie has won countless fans.

When shopping for sweet potatoes, be sure to select the orange-fleshed variety. Along with being a bit sweeter and more flavorful, orange-fleshed sweet potatoes look spectacular in a single-crust pie.

INGREDIENTS

1¾ pounds sweet potatoes, whole and with skins on

One 9-inch piecrust, homemade (page 20) or store-bought

4 tablespoons unsalted butter, melted

¾ cup firmly packed light brown sugar

2 large eggs, beaten

1 teaspoon vanilla extract

1 cup milk

¾ teaspoon ground cinnamon

½ teaspoon salt

¼ teaspoon ground nutmeg

¼ teaspoon ground ginger

Whipped cream, optional, for serving

DIRECTIONS

1. Bring a large saucepan or small stockpot filled with salted water to a boil. Add the sweet potatoes and cook until very tender, 20 to 25 minutes.

2. Drain the potatoes and allow them to cool.

3. Preheat the oven to 400°F.

4. Line a 9-inch pie pan with the piecrust. Prick the crust with a fork. Fill the bottom of the crust with pie weights or dried beans.

5. Place the piecrust in the oven and bake for 10 to 15 minutes, until the edges begin to turn golden. Remove the crust from the oven and remove the weights. Allow the crust to cool on a wire rack.

6. Once the sweet potatoes have cooled enough that you can comfortably work with them, peel off and discard their skins. Cut the potatoes into chunks and place them in the bowl of a blender or food processor. Puree until smooth and creamy, about 1 minute.

7. Add the butter, brown sugar, eggs, vanilla, milk, cinnamon, salt, nutmeg, and ginger to the potatoes and pulse until well combined, less than 1 minute.

8. Pour the sweet potato filling into the crust and bake for 20 minutes. After 20 minutes reduce the oven temperature to 325°F. If the edges of the crust are starting to brown, gently cover them with a pie guard or strips of aluminum foil.

9. Bake the pie for an additional 20 minutes or until the filling has set but is not brown or cracking. You want the center of the filling to jiggle slightly when you wiggle the pan.

10. Remove the pie from the oven and cool on a wire rack. Serve warm or cold with an optional topping of whipped cream.

Molten Mince Pie

SERVES 8

Redolent with the warm scents of cinnamon, cloves, apples, and raisins, this pie used to be made with minced beef or suet. Hence the name mince pie or, as my parents called it, mincemeat pie. In my version, mince refers to the bite-sized pieces of dates, apples, raisins, sultanas, and currants in the filling.

You can make this aromatic pie with two homemade crusts or with two 9-inch store-bought deep-dish piecrusts. If you opt for store-bought, remember to follow the instructions on the packaging for defrosting and baking the crusts.

INGREDIENTS

¼ cup pitted dates, chopped

1 cup raisins

1 cup golden raisins (sultanas)

1 cup currants

2 pounds Granny Smith apples, peeled and diced

Zest and juice of 1 lemon

1-inch piece of ginger, peeled and grated

½ teaspoon ground cinnamon

½ teaspoon allspice

½ teaspoon ground cloves

¼ teaspoon ground nutmeg

⅓ cup orange marmalade

½ cup dark brown (muscovado) sugar

2 tablespoons cognac

Two 9-inch piecrusts, homemade (page 20) or store-bought deep-dish crusts

Homemade whipped cream or vanilla ice cream for serving, optional

DIRECTIONS

1. Place the dates, raisins, sultanas, currants, apples, lemon zest and juice, ginger, cinnamon, allspice, cloves, nutmeg, marmalade, sugar, and cognac in a large saucepan. Bring the ingredients to a simmer over medium-low heat. Allow the ingredients to cook for 10 to 15 minutes or until all the liquid has been dissolved.

2. Preheat the oven to 425°F.

3. Line a 9-inch pie pan with one piecrust. Evenly spread the mince over the crust and smooth out the top.

4. Wet the edge of the crust with a smidgen of water and then place the remaining crust over the mince. Using your fingers, press the edges of the crusts together.

5. Prick the top of the crust with either a fork or sharp knife.

6. Bake for 10 minutes at 425°F. Lower the temperature to 350°F and bake for an additional 35 to 45 minutes or until the crust is golden.

7. Remove the pie from the oven and completely cool on a wire rack. Serve with homemade whipped cream or vanilla ice cream.

Sublime Strawberry Pavlova

SERVES 8

Named for the Russian ballerina Anna Pavlova, who had visited New Zealand in 1926, this elegant, meringue-based dessert has sparked debate in the baking world. New Zealanders claim it as their country's creation. So, too, do Australians, who point out that Anna Pavlova had also gone to their land. What isn't in dispute is my love of this dessert. While traveling in New Zealand, I ended almost every evening meal with a towering mound of silken meringue, pillowy whipped cream, and juicy fruit.

Back at home I spent weeks making and comparing pavlova recipes. Through all that eating and baking and eating, I learned the trick for making an extra moist pavlova. About 30 minutes before serving I layer the fruit over the meringue and whipped cream and allow the two to absorb the fruit's ruby red juices. The result is an utterly sublime dessert.

INGREDIENTS

FOR THE MERINGUE

4 large egg whites, at room temperature

1 teaspoon vanilla extract

½ teaspoon lemon juice

¾ cup granulated sugar

FOR THE FRUIT TOPPING

2 cups sliced strawberries

3 tablespoons granulated sugar

Juice of ½ lime

FOR THE WHIPPED CREAM

1 cup heavy cream

¼ cup granulated sugar

½ teaspoon vanilla extract

DIRECTIONS

1. Preheat the oven to 350°F. Line a baking sheet with parchment paper and set aside.

2. For the meringue, place the egg whites in a large bowl. Using an electric mixer, beat the egg whites until soft peaks form.

3. Add the vanilla extract and lemon juice and beat to incorporate.

4. Adding the sugar a spoonful at a time, continue to beat the egg whites until stiff, glossy peaks form.

5. Spoon the meringue onto the prepared baking sheet and shape it into an even circle. If, like me, your circles tend to come out lopsided, use my small cheat and mound the meringue onto a parchment round that you've placed on top of the original parchment sheet. Perfect circles every time!

6. Place the baking sheet in the oven, lower the temperature to 225°F and bake for 1 hour. After 1 hour, turn off the oven and peek in on your pavlova. It should look firm, even a bit crackly, but not browned. As long as it hasn't browned at all, allow the meringue to cool for at least 1 hour or overnight in the oven. If it has darkened ever so slightly in color, remove it from the oven to cool. You want the meringue to be white, not beige or browning.

(Continued)

7. When you're ready to make the topping and assemble the pavlova, place the strawberries in a small saucepan with the sugar and lime juice. Simmer them over medium-low until the berries begin to release their juices, 3 to 5 minutes.

8. Strain the berries, returning any excess liquid to the pan. Bring the liquid to a boil over medium-high and then reduce the heat to medium-low. Allow the liquid to simmer until thickened, 3 to 5 minutes.

9. As the liquid is reducing, make the whipped cream. Place the cream, sugar, and vanilla extract in a large bowl. Using an electric mixer or hand whisk, beat until soft peaks form. Once you have soft peaks, your whipped cream is ready.

10. To assemble, spread the whipped cream over the meringue, leaving a bare edge of 1 to 2 inches

11. Thirty minutes before serving spoon the fruit over the whipped cream. Drizzle the reduced strawberry juice over the dessert. Slice and serve.

Sticky Toffee Puddings

SERVES 8

I first encountered this astonishing dessert on a wintry night in a damp and drafty medieval castle turned bed & breakfast on the outskirts of Edinburgh, Scotland. After a meal of wild, Scottish salmon and mashed turnips in the B&B's frigid dining room, I decided to indulge in a final, warming course. If I was going to shiver to death in my cold, blanketless bed, at least it would be after I had enjoyed one last sweet. What an incredible sweet it was! Steeped in a toasty toffee sauce, this warm, moist, cakelike pudding was unlike anything I had ever eaten.

Although I first tried sticky toffee pudding in Scotland, this hearty dessert originated in England's Lake District. Nowhere nearly as old as the castle in which I ate it, the original recipe dates back to the 1970s.

INGREDIENTS

FOR THE PUDDINGS

1¼ cups chopped pitted dates

½ teaspoon vanilla extract

1 teaspoon baking soda

1 cup boiling water

5 tablespoons unsalted butter, at room temperature

1 cup firmly packed light brown sugar

4 large eggs

2 cups all-purpose flour

½ teaspoon baking soda

¼ teaspoon salt

FOR THE TOFFEE SAUCE

4 tablespoons unsalted butter

⅔ cup turbinado sugar

1 teaspoon vanilla extract

¼ cup milk

Whipped cream, optional, for serving

DIRECTIONS

1. Preheat the oven to 350°F. Grease and flour 8 ramekins or an 8-inch square baking dish and set aside.

2. Place the dates, vanilla, baking soda, and boiling water in a large saucepan over medium heat. Boil, stirring occasionally, for 15 minutes. Note that the baking soda will cause the mixture to foam, so stir frequently to avoid overflows.

3. After 15 minutes, remove the pan from the heat and allow the ingredients to cool.

4. Using an electric mixer, beat the butter until creamy, 2 to 3 minutes. Add the brown sugar and beat again until well incorporated. Add the eggs one at a time, beating well, and scraping down the sides of the bowl after each addition.

5. Sift together the flour, baking soda, and salt. Beat the flour mixture into the liquids in two additions, scraping down the bowl after each time. Add the date mixture and stir to combine.

6. Spoon equal amounts of batter into the ramekins, filling each to two-thirds from the top, or spoon the batter into the baking dish. If

(Continued)

using ramekins, place them on a baking sheet and bake for 25 to 30 minutes, until a toothpick inserted into the centers comes out clean. If using a baking dish, bake for 35 minutes or until a toothpick inserted into the center comes out clean.

7. While the puddings are baking, make the toffee sauce. Place the butter, sugar, vanilla, and milk in a saucepan over medium heat. Stir frequently until the ingredients are well combined and resemble a thick, brownish sauce, 7 to 9 minutes. Remove the pan from the heat and set aside.

8. Reduce the oven temperature to 300°F and remove the puddings. Using a thin-bladed, sharp knife, loosen the edges of the puddings and invert them on a platter. If you've made these in a baking dish, loosen the edges and then slice and place equal portions of pudding onto the platter.

9. With your knife, score the top of each with a small x.

10. Pour a third of the warm toffee sauce into the ramekins or baking dish. Leaving the scored side up, return the puddings to their sauce-lined vessel(s) and pour another third of the toffee sauce over them.

11. Return the puddings to the oven for 5 minutes so that the puddings absorb the sauce.

12. Remove the puddings from the oven and cool for 5 minutes. As the puddings cool, reheat the remaining toffee sauce.

13. Using your thin, sharp knife, loosen the puddings from the ramekins or baking dish. Invert each pudding onto a plate. Pour the warmed toffee sauce over each and top with an optional dollop of whipped cream. Serve warm.

Toothsome Pumpkin-Ginger Trifle

SERVES 8 TO 10

A British dessert from medieval times, trifle traditionally consists of liquor-soaked sponge cake, fruit, custard, and whipped cream. In this instance I replace the sponge cake with cookies and incorporate the fruit into the custard. The result is an opulent treat.

You can make the pumpkin custard up to two days in advance. Press a piece of plastic wrap onto the custard and refrigerate until you're ready to assemble your trifle. Once you've put together the trifle, refrigerate and allow the ginger snaps to soften, the flavors to come together, and the trifle to transform into the luxurious dessert that it is. You can refrigerate the trifle from 1 to 12 hours. Keep in mind that the longer the refrigeration, the more sumptuous the trifle. Before serving, sprinkle the crystallized ginger over the top.

INGREDIENTS

FOR THE CUSTARD

2 ¼ cups unsweetened pure pumpkin

3 large eggs

2 egg yolks

1 cup light whipping cream

2 cups milk

1 tablespoon vanilla extract

¾ cup granulated sugar

2 teaspoons ground cinnamon

½ teaspoon ground ginger

¼ teaspoon ground nutmeg

¼ teaspoon allspice

Pinch of ground cloves

Pinch of salt

3 tablespoons cornstarch

FOR THE BASE

⅓ cup spiced rum

¼ cup granulated sugar

1 tablespoon vanilla extract

16 to 24 ginger snaps

1 cup roughly chopped candied pecans

FOR THE WHIPPED CREAM TOPPING

1¼ cups heavy cream

1 teaspoon vanilla extract

3 tablespoons granulated sugar

2 to 3 tablespoons minced crystallized ginger

DIRECTIONS

1. In a large, nonstick frying pan over medium heat, cook the pumpkin for 5 minutes. You want most of the liquid from the pumpkin to evaporate. Remove the pan from the heat and set aside.

2. To make the pumpkin custard, place the eggs, egg yolks, cream, milk, vanilla, sugar, cinnamon, ginger, nutmeg, allspice, cloves, salt, and cornstarch in a saucepan over medium heat. Cook, stirring constantly, until the ingredients have thickened, 6 to 8 minutes. Whisk in the cooked pumpkin and simmer for another 2 to 3 minutes. When finished, the custard will coat the back of a spoon.

3. Remove the pan from the heat and allow the custard to cool slightly. Once it has cooled,

(Continued)

cover the top with a piece of plastic wrap, pressing the wrap onto the custard, and refrigerate.

4. When you're ready to make the base and assemble the trifle, whisk the rum, sugar, and vanilla in a small saucepan over low heat until the sugar has dissolved, 1 to 2 minutes.

5. Place 2 to 3 overlapping layers of ginger snaps on the bottom of a large, deep, glass bowl. Pour the warmed rum over the cookies and allow them to absorb the liquor.

6. At this point make the whipped cream. In a large bowl and using an electric mixer, beat together the cream and vanilla until thickened, 1 to 2 minutes. Add the sugar and continue beating until firm peaks form. Set the bowl aside.

7. Spread the candied pecans over the ginger snaps. Spoon the pumpkin custard over the nuts and then spread the whipped cream over the custard. Sprinkle the crystallized ginger over top. Refrigerate for at least 1 hour. Serve chilled.

Sleek and Tasty Tiramisu

SERVES 6 TO 8

It's my ending to every Italian restaurant meal and one of the creamiest desserts around. Tiramisu gets its ethereal texture from layers of whipped mascarpone cheese, espresso- and liqueur-soaked sponge cake or ladyfinger cookies, and cocoa-dusted whipped cream.

Because we mastered sponge cake in our Everyone Loves Lamingtons recipe (page 130) and created it again in My Favorite Victoria Sponge (page 132), I encourage you to make your tiramisu base from homemade sponge. However, if you don't have time to bake, you can substitute good quality, store-bought ladyfingers for the homemade sponge cake.

INGREDIENTS

1 sponge cake (page 132) or 14 to 18 lady-finger cookies

3 large eggs, separated

½ cup granulated sugar

2 teaspoons vanilla extract

12 ounces mascarpone cheese, at room temperature

¾ cup (6 ounces) brewed espresso or strong coffee, at room temperature

2 tablespoons coffee-flavored rum or liqueur

2 to 3 ounces semisweet chocolate, grated

Unsweetened cocoa powder, for dusting

DIRECTIONS

1. Preheat the oven to 350°F.

2. If using a sponge cake for your base, slice the cake into 2-inch-long and wide and ½-inch-thick pieces. Place the sponge cake or cookies on a large baking sheet.

3. Toast the cake or cookies in the oven for 1 to 2 minutes. Turn the pieces over and toast for 2 to 3 minutes, until firm and golden in color. Remove the pan from the oven and allow the cake or cookies to cool.

4. Bring a saucepan filled halfway with water to a boil. Set a mixing bowl on top of the saucepan. Add the egg yolks and sugar to the bowl and whisk until the temperature on a deep-fry or candy thermometer reaches 160°F. Note that if you have a double boiler, feel free to use this instead of the mixing bowl and pan of hot water.

5. Remove the bowl from the saucepan and set aside. Whisking periodically, allow the ingredients to cool for 10 to 15 minutes.

6. In a separate bowl beat the egg whites until soft peaks form. Add the vanilla extract and beat again until stiff, glossy peaks form.

7. Place the mascarpone in a bowl. Fold in the egg yolk mixture followed by the whipped egg whites. Set aside.

8. In a shallow dish or bowl stir together the espresso and rum.

(Continued)

9. Dunk a cookie or cake strip into the coffee mixture until saturated. Place it in the bottom of a serving bowl or decorative baking dish. Repeat until you have a layer of extremely moist cookies or cake. Spread a layer of the mascarpone cheese mixture over top. Sprinkle some of the grated chocolate over the mascarpone.

10. Repeat dipping and layering until you have spread the final layer of mascarpone filling. Depending on the size of your bowl, you could have one, two, or even three layers of mascarpone.

11. Sprinkle the grated chocolate and then sift the cocoa powder over the last mascarpone layer. Cover the tiramisu and refrigerate for a minimum of 1 hour. For the most luscious results, refrigerate the tiramisu for 24 hours before serving.

Velvety Cookies, Pastries, and Breads

WHAT DO THE FOLLOWING COOKIES, PASTRIES, and breads have in common? Besides being baked goods, they all possess the delightfully luscious, tender, and/or juicy texture that we crave. From glistening coconut macaroons to satiny cranberry- and chocolate-studded panettone and tender bars, buns, rolls, and breads in between, these sweets dazzle with their moist luxuriousness.

As with cakes, pies, and puddings, the ingredients featured in a cookie, pastry, or bread will influence its consistency. A smidgen of milk added to cookie dough will make it tender. Bumping up the amount of flour slightly will produce a similar result in cookie dough, but doing that with pastry dough will make it dry and crumbly.

How long you mix your ingredients will also impact the texture of your baked goods. Whatever you do, don't overmix your dough. When you stir or beat cookie dough beyond the recommended time, you add too much air to the batter. An overly aerated dough results in crisp and flat, rather than moist and fat, cookies. When you overmix pastry dough, you end up with gummy pastries. Follow the recipe instructions and mix for the specified amount of time. Do the same for baking temperatures and times.

As I mention in this book's Introduction, you should cool your baked goods completely before storing them in airtight containers. If you put warm cookies and the like in closed containers, condensation will form. Your baked goods will turn soggy and, if stored long enough, mold. This is why you have to cool your treats first.

To keep your sweets soft and moist, add a slice or two of bread to the container. Over time the bread will release moisture and replenish your baked goods, giving them that desirable texture. More information can be found in Keeping Cookies Moist on page 165.

Mmmm . . . Coconut Macaroons

MAKES 2 DOZEN COOKIES

Macaroons and macarons. Take away a vowel and you end up with an entirely different treat. In recent years, consumers have been fixated on the fussy, cream-filled macaron with a single "o." Long before the macaron craze there were the moist, domed cookies known as macaroons.

Macaroons contain only a few ingredients. Yet, when combined together, they create an exquisite, sweet cookie. Initially, macaroons were served as a light snack alongside liqueurs and wine. Today they remain a nice little pick-me-up in the middle of the day as well as a pleasurable way to end a meal.

INGREDIENTS

¼ cup granulated sugar

3⅓ cups sweetened shredded coconut

Pinch of salt

2 tablespoons unsalted butter, melted

3 large egg whites

DIRECTIONS

1. Preheat the oven to 350°F. Line two baking sheets with parchment paper.

2. In a large bowl mix together the sugar, coconut, and salt. Pour the melted butter over the coconut and stir until coated.

3. In a separate bowl whisk the egg whites until white, foamy, and roughly double in volume, about 1 minute. Add them to the coconut and stir until well combined.

4. Using a tablespoon or a small disher or cookie dough scoop, form equal-sized balls and place them in rows on the parchment-lined baking sheets. Bake for 15 to 20 minutes, until golden brown. Allow the cookies to cool for 5 minutes before removing them from the pans and cooling them completely on wire racks.

Gooey Chocolate S'mores Cookies

MAKES 4½ DOZEN COOKIES

Sweet without being cloying, chocolaty without being too rich, these cookies strike the perfect balance. Dotted with chunks of graham cracker, chocolate, and marshmallow, the moist, cocoa-enriched dough is far more complex and appealing than the usual double chocolate chip cookie. As with its campfire namesake, this cookie is so good that it will leave you hankering for "some more." Yep, that's how s'mores got their name. You can't just eat one graham cracker, chocolate bar, toasted marshmallow combo. You always want "s'more."

INGREDIENTS

3 cups semisweet chocolate chips

1 stick (8 tablespoons) unsalted butter

1½ cups all-purpose flour

3 tablespoons unsweetened cocoa

1½ teaspoons baking powder

½ teaspoon salt

3 large eggs

¾ cup firmly packed light brown sugar

½ cup granulated sugar

1 teaspoon vanilla extract

¾ cup (4 to 5 sheets) roughly crumbled graham crackers

¾ cup mini marshmallows

DIRECTIONS

1. Preheat the oven to 350°F. Line two baking sheets with parchment paper and set aside.

2. In a double boiler on the stove or in a glass bowl in the microwave, melt half of the chocolate chips and all the butter, stirring together periodically until the chocolate has fully melted. Set aside to cool.

3. In a large bowl sift together the flour, cocoa, baking powder, and salt.

4. Using either an electric stand or hand mixer, beat together the eggs, sugars, and vanilla until light in color, 1 to 2 minutes. Scrape down the sides of the bowl and then add the cooled, melted chocolate, beating until well combined.

5. Scrape down the sides of the bowl again and add the flour mixture. Beat until the flour is fully incorporated and a soft dough has formed, 1 to 2 minutes.

6. Add the remaining chocolate chips, crumbled graham crackers, and mini marshmallows and stir to combine.

7. Shape the dough into 1-inch balls and place the balls on the parchment paper–lined baking sheets, leaving an inch or so between each cookie. Bake for 10 to 12 minutes, until the cookies are firm. Remove the pans from the oven and allow the cookies to cool for 2 to 3 minutes before removing them from the pan and cooling them completely on a wire rack. Repeat until all the cookies have been baked.

Keeping Cookies Moist

If, in spite of your best efforts, you open your airtight container and discover that your cookies have become dry and/or brittle, don't despair. In this rare instance I will advise you to do what my mother did and drape a few slices of bread on top of your treats. Worried about bread crumbs clinging to your cookies? If you have a terra-cotta sugar saver, you can use that instead of bread. Soak the sugar saver in water for 15 minutes and then pat it dry before adding it to the cookie container.

Once the bread or sugar saver is tucked inside, close the container and allow your goodies to absorb some of that moisture. Depending on how soft and pliant you want your cookies to be, this could take anywhere from 45 minutes to several hours.

Halfway through this process, you should reposition the cookies so that the ones on the top move to the bottom and vice versa. By rotating the cookies, you'll end up with a more uniform consistency.

Once you're ready to consume the cookies, remove the bread or sugar saver. Place the cookies on a decorative platter and serve.

Sumptuous Brown Butter–Butterscotch Cookies

MAKES 3½ DOZEN COOKIES

To make the nutty brown butter in this recipe, swirl unsalted butter in a saucepan over medium heat until the water in the butter evaporates, the butter turns dark gold, and brown flecks of milk solids form. At that point remove the pan from the heat and either strain out the brown flecks or leave them in. That's it. That's all there is to creating brown butter.

Because you have removed the water from the butter, you will need to add liquid back to your dough. One or two tablespoons of milk will do the trick. If you don't include that smidgen of milk, your cookies will be crisp and crumbly and not the velvety texture that we want.

INGREDIENTS

16 tablespoons (2 sticks) unsalted butter, cut into pieces

¾ cup firmly packed light brown sugar

1 teaspoon vanilla extract

2 tablespoons milk

2 large eggs, at room temperature

2⅓ cups all-purpose flour

1 teaspoon salt

1 teaspoon baking soda

¾ cup plus 2 tablespoons butterscotch chips

DIRECTIONS

1. Preheat the oven to 350°F. Cut and place parchment paper on two baking sheets. Set aside.

2. In a medium-sized pan melt the butter over medium-low heat. Continue cooking and swirling the pan over the heat. During this time the butter will foam, possibly pop, and slowly settle, 4 to 5 minutes.

3. Continue cooking and swirling the pan for another 2 to 3 minutes. During this time the butter will turn dark gold in color and brown specks, which are milk solids, will form.

4. Remove the butter from the heat and allow it to cool slightly before stirring in the sugar, vanilla, and milk. Cool the liquids to room temperature and then add the eggs, whisking to combine.

5. In a large bowl mix together the flour, salt, and baking soda. Add the liquids to the flour and mix well. Add the butterscotch chips and stir until combined.

6. Using a tablespoon or cookie dough scoop or disher, shape 1 tablespoon of dough into a ball and place it on the baking sheet. Continue shaping and placing the cookies about 1 inch apart. Repeat until all the dough has been used.

7. Bake for 15 to 18 minutes, until the cookies have browned on their bottoms. Remove the cookies from the baking sheets and cool on wire racks. For best results, store in airtight containers and consume within 3 days.

VELVETY COOKIES, PASTRIES, AND BREADS

LUSCIOUS, TENDER, JUICY

Triple-the-Pleasure, Triple-the-Chocolate Brownies

MAKES 12 LARGE OR 24 SMALL BROWNIES

An enduring favorite, brownies woo us with their moist, fudgy interiors, crisp, paper-thin crusts, and intense, chocolaty taste. Some bakers refer to these yummy cookies as bars of chocolate stitched together by flour and eggs, while others consider them a socially acceptable method for consuming large quantities of chocolate. Both aptly describe the decadent Triple-the-Pleasure, Triple-the-Chocolate Brownies.

INGREDIENTS

6 ounces bittersweet chocolate, chopped

6 ounces semisweet morsels

9 tablespoons unsalted butter

1 tablespoon vanilla extract

1 cup granulated sugar

2 large eggs, beaten

⅔ cup all-purpose flour

1½ teaspoons baking powder

½ teaspoon salt

3 ounces white chocolate chips

DIRECTIONS

1. Preheat the oven to 350°F. Grease a 13-by-9-inch baking pan and set aside.

2. Using either a double boiler on your stove or a small heatproof bowl in a microwave, melt half of the bittersweet chocolate and semisweet morsels, and all the butter together. Stir until the ingredients are fully incorporated. Set aside to cool.

3. In a large bowl whisk together the vanilla, sugar, and eggs until just mixed.

4. In another bowl whisk together the flour, baking powder, and salt.

5. Once the melted chocolate has cooled, stir it into the egg mixture.

6. Fold the flour into the chocolate-egg mixture. Add the remaining bittersweet and semisweet morsels and the white chocolate and stir to combine.

7. Evenly spread the brownie batter in the prepared pan and bake for 28 to 30 minutes. When the brownies have puffed up and feel slightly firm, they are done. Do not overbake them.

8. Remove the pan from the oven and allow the brownies to cool completely on a wire rack. Slice into 12 large or 24 small brownies.

Silky Hungarian Cherry Squares

MAKES 12 LARGE CHERRY SQUARES

At the end of a long week in journalism school, I used to trudge a few blocks south to the crowded, dimly lit Hungarian Pastry Shop on Manhattan's Upper West Side. There I would treat myself to a black coffee and the soft, plump baked good known as a cherry square. Black coffee I could get anywhere. A square of silken dough packed with tender, sweetly tart cherries was a rare indulgence.

After grad school I traveled to Hungary and ordered these cherry-filled pastries at every café and coffee house I visited. None were as soft and dreamy as the ones I'd eaten after class on those late Friday afternoons. The following recipe is my tribute to those one-of-a-kind treats.

INGREDIENTS

FOR THE DOUGH

1 stick (8 tablespoons) unsalted butter, cold, cut into chunks

2 cups plus 2 tablespoons all-purpose flour

¼ teaspoon salt

½ cup confectioners' sugar

1 large egg

1½ teaspoons vanilla extract

½ cup sour cream

FOR THE FILLING

Three 15-ounce cans pitted whole cherries in water, drained with 2 tablespoons of liquid reserved

1 cup granulated sugar

¼ teaspoon ground cinnamon

1 teaspoon almond extract

3 tablespoons cornstarch

½ cup ground blanched almonds

FOR THE TOPPING

1 large egg

1 teaspoon water

Confectioners' sugar for dusting

DIRECTIONS

1. For the dough, using a pastry cutter or sturdy fork, cut the butter into the flour in a large bowl. Add the salt and sugar and stir to combine.

2. In a small bowl whisk together the egg, vanilla, and sour cream and stir them into the flour. The final dough will be crumbly and not completely formed.

3. Put the dough on a clean work surface and knead until a soft, smooth dough forms, 4 to 6 minutes. If you have a stand mixer with a dough hook, place the dough in the bowl of the mixer and knead on high until a soft, smooth dough forms, 1 to 2 minutes.

4. Divide the dough in half and shape into two balls. Cover each with plastic wrap and refrigerate for 30 minutes.

5. As the dough is chilling, make the cherry filling. In a medium saucepan bring the cherries, 2 tablespoons of cherry liquid, sugar, cinnamon, and almond extract to a simmer over medium-low heat. Once the liquid starts to bubble, sift the cornstarch over the cherries and stir to combine. Cook until the liquids have turned to a thick sauce, 2 to 3 minutes.

6. Preheat the oven to 375°F.

7. Place one of the two balls of dough on a lightly floured work surface. Roll it out until it's slightly larger than 8-by-11½ inches.

8. Fold the dough in half lengthwise and center it into an 8-by-11½-by-2-inch baking dish. Unfold and lightly pat the dough into place.

9. Roll out the second ball of dough so that it is 8-by-11½ inches. Set aside.

10. Evenly spread the almonds, followed by the cherries, over the bottom of the dough.

11. Position the top crust over the cherry filling. If you have any excess dough hanging over the edge of the dish, slice off and discard it. Pinch the edges of the bottom and top crusts together.

12. To make the egg wash, whisk together the egg and water. Brush this over the top crust. Using a fork, prick several holes in the crust.

13. Bake for 35 to 40 minutes, until lightly browned on top. Remove the pan from the oven and place it on a wire rack. Sift confectioners' sugar over the top.

14. Allow the dessert to cool completely before slicing it into 12 squares.

What Sour Cream Brings to Baking

Sour cream is light cream that, through the addition of lactic acid, has soured. Possessing around 20 percent fat, it brings a luscious texture and tangy taste to a range of baked goods. Because of its high fat content and acidity, sour cream adds more moisture to batters and doughs than milk. Cakes containing sour cream possess a creamier, finer crumb. Pastries made with sour cream are tenderer.

In recipes calling for sour cream, use full-fat or, in a pinch, reduced-fat sour cream. Avoid nonfat sour cream, which will not give your baked goods that moist creaminess. When replacing whole milk with sour cream, you can do a 1:1 swap.

Best Ever Baklava

MAKES 16 PIECES

Recipe courtesy of Vasiliki Kolovos.

For centuries a dispute has existed over who invented the nutty, honeyed, phyllo-based treat known as baklava. Was it Turkey or was it Greece who created this glistening jewel of a sweet?

My first bite of baklava happened in the Greek-American home of one of my closest childhood friends, Dr. Nikoleta Kolovos. Because of this introduction, and because my baklava recipe comes directly from her mom, Vasiliki Kolovos, I have to side with Greece. After all, if it weren't for Mrs. Kolovos's opulent Greek baked goods and her enthusiasm for sharing recipes and food, I may never have developed a passion for global cuisines or cooking.

Because phyllo can be a bit temperamental, take a moment to read Working with Phyllo Dough on page 174.

INGREDIENTS

FOR THE BAKLAVA

1 pound (4 cups) finely chopped walnuts

¼ cup granulated sugar

1 teaspoon ground cinnamon

¼ teaspoon ground cloves

1 pound store-bought phyllo, thawed according to the package's instructions

1½ sticks (12 tablespoons) unsalted butter, melted

16 whole cloves

FOR THE SYRUP

2 cups granulated sugar

2 cups water

1 cinnamon stick

A few whole cloves

Peel of 1 orange

1 teaspoon vanilla extract

½ cup honey

DIRECTIONS

1. Preheat the oven to 325°F. Grease a 9-by-13-inch baking pan and set aside.

2. In a medium bowl mix the walnuts, sugar, cinnamon, and cloves together. Set aside.

3. Gently lift and place a sheet of phyllo in your prepared baking pan. Brush a thin layer of butter over the top of the sheet and then place another sheet of phyllo on top of it. Butter and layer until you have five sheets of buttered phyllo.

4. Spread one-third of the walnut mixture over the top sheet. Cover the nuts with three sheets of buttered phyllo. Spread another third of the walnut mixture over the top sheet. Repeat until you've used the last third of walnuts.

5. Cover the last layer of walnuts with five buttered phyllo sheets. Tuck the edges of the phyllo into the sides of the pan.

6. Refrigerate the baklava for 15 minutes.

7. After 15 minutes remove the pan from the refrigerator. Using a sharp, serrated knife, mark the baklava into square- or diamond-

(Continued)

shaped pieces. Be sure to cut into the top layer of phyllo and nuts and no further. You'll completely slice the baklava after it's finished baking.

8. Insert a clove into the center of each piece. Sprinkle a little water over each.

9. Bake until golden brown, 45 to 60 minutes.

10. As your baklava is baking, make the syrup. Combine the sugar, water, cinnamon stick, cloves, orange peel, and vanilla in a small saucepan. Bring the ingredients to boil over medium-high heat. Boil for 5 to 10 minutes, until the liquid begins to reduce.

11. Remove the cinnamon stick, cloves, and orange peel. Add the honey and stir to combine. Continue to boil for 10 to 15 minutes, until the syrup is thick enough to coat the back of a spoon. You will have roughly 2 cups of bronze-colored syrup.

12. Remove the syrup from the heat and allow it to cool. Note that you can make the syrup a day in advance and refrigerate it. Allow it to reach room temperature before using.

13. Once the baklava has finished baking, remove the pan from the oven and place it on a wire rack to cool for 15 minutes.

14. Using your sharp, serrated knife, finish cutting into your scored baklava. Make sure that you slice all the way down to the bottom of the pan. That way, all the layers will absorb the syrup. Plus, you won't struggle to remove pieces that are still connected to each other.

15. Pour the syrup over the baklava, evenly covering each piece. Allow the baklava to soak up the syrup for at least 4 hours. Ideally, cover and refrigerate the baklava overnight.

16. Serve at room temperature.

Working with Phyllo Dough

Open a package of frozen phyllo and you'll find a stack of pale, feathery light sheets reminiscent of the pages of a book. Phyllo's name comes from the Greek word for "leaf," which is a fitting description for this fragile, tissue paper–thin dough.

Because this dough dries out quickly, you should take precautions to ensure that it stays moist. First off, when defrosting frozen phyllo, leave the dough in its plastic wrap to thaw. That way, it remains in a moist environment.

As the phyllo is defrosting, make the filling. By doing this now, you can quickly assemble your phyllo-based treat and reduce the amount of time that the dough is exposed to the air.

Once the dough has thawed and you're ready to use it, wet a clean dish towel and ring out any excess water. You want the towel to be damp, not dripping. Lay the towel over the sheets that you won't immediately work with. Covering them with a damp cloth will stop them from losing moisture.

Another way to prevent dry phyllo is to steer clear of hot rooms and direct sunlight. Placing phyllo in either environment will cause it to desiccate quickly.

Remember to brush melted butter over each sheet of phyllo that you use. If the phyllo tears as you're doing this, don't panic. Just paste it back together or patch it with scraps of dough and a bit of melted butter.

VELVETY COOKIES, PASTRIES, AND BREADS

Delectable Peach Danish

MAKES 12 DANISHES

The laminated yeast dough used for Delectable Peach Danish is sometimes referred to as puff dough. It's quite similar to puff pastry. Puff dough contains fewer layers of butter than puff pastry, but it still possesses that supple texture and heavenly taste.

It will take a bit of time to make your own laminated yeast dough. Once you have mixed the dough with the cold butter, you should let it rest in your refrigerator for several hours, if not overnight. After that, though, you can quickly form and fill your Danishes. As for the filling, if you prefer raspberry, strawberry, or another fruit preserve over peach, feel free to use that in your Danishes instead. Likewise, if you'd prefer to use a puff pastry for this dessert, you can use the recipe for Homemade Puff Pastry (page 22).

INGREDIENTS

FOR THE SPONGE

1 large egg

¾ cup plus 1 tablespoon warm water

1½ cups all-purpose flour

1½ tablespoons granulated sugar

1⅛ teaspoons active dry yeast

1 teaspoon vanilla extract

1 tablespoon unsalted butter, melted

FOR THE DOUGH

1½ cups all-purpose flour

1½ tablespoons granulated sugar

1 tablespoon milk

½ teaspoon salt

FOR THE BUTTER

14 tablespoons unsalted butter, cold

3 tablespoons all-purpose flour

FOR THE EGG WASH

1 large egg

1 tablespoon water

FOR THE FILLING

½ cup good-quality peach preserves

FOR THE GLAZE (OPTIONAL)

1 cup sifted confectioners' sugar

1 to 2 tablespoons warm water

(Continued)

DIRECTIONS

1. To make the sponge, whisk the egg and warm water together in a large bowl.

2. Stir in half of the flour and half of the sugar and all the yeast. Once the ingredients are combined, cover the bowl with plastic wrap and place it in a warm spot for 30 minutes, until it begins to bubble and rise.

3. As the sponge is developing, combine the dough ingredients: In a large bowl stir together the flour, sugar, milk, and salt. Set this aside.

4. Once the sponge has begun to rise and bubble, about 30 minutes, add the remaining ¾ cup sponge flour and 2¼ teaspoons sponge sugar, the vanilla extract, and melted butter to the sponge bowl, and stir to combine.

5. Add the sponge to the dough mixture and stir until you have created a soft dough. Form this into a ball and place on either a lightly floured work surface or in the bowl of an electric stand mixer fitted with a dough hook.

6. Knead the dough until it becomes elastic in texture, about 7 to 10 minutes. Form it into a ball, cover the ball with plastic wrap and refrigerate for 30 minutes.

7. While the dough is resting, put the cold butter and 3 tablespoons flour in either the bowl of your stand mixer, which is now fitted with a beater, or a traditional mixing bowl. Beat together until smooth and creamy, 2 to 3 minutes.

8. Using your hands, shape the butter mixture into a $^1/_8$-inch-high square. Cover it with plastic wrap and refrigerate for 30 minutes.

9. To finish making your laminated yeast dough, remove the dough from the refrigerator and put it on a floured work surface. Using a lightly floured rolling pin, roll out the dough into a 12-inch square.

10. Remove the butter from the refrigerator, unwrap and place it at an angle in the center of the dough. It should look like a diamond in the center of the square.

11. Fold the edges of the dough over the butter; it should look like an envelope. Using your fingers, seal these edges.

12. Place your rolling pin in the center of the square and roll out a large rectangle that's roughly 15-by-20 inches. Fold the rectangle into a square and seal the edges before rolling it out into a rectangle again.

13. Brush off any excess flour. Cover the dough with plastic wrap and refrigerate for 30 minutes.

14. Remove the dough from the refrigerator and place it on a lightly floured work surface. Fold the dough into a square, roll it out into a rectangle, and then fold it into a square again. Cover the dough and refrigerate it for at least 2 hours or overnight.

15. Grease two baking sheets and set aside. Whisk together the egg and water for the egg wash.

16. Remove the dough from the refrigerator and place it on a lightly floured work surface. Using a rolling pin, roll it out until you have a rectangle that is the width of your rolling pin and about 1½ times in length.

17. Using a thin, sharp-bladed knife, slice the dough into 12 equally sized squares, each roughly 5-by-5 inches. The easiest way to do this is to slice the dough into thirds horizontally and then slice four equally sized, vertical rows.

18. Place one square with a pointed end facing you; it should look like a diamond. Drop 1 to 2 teaspoons of preserves in the center of the square.

19. Bring the two pointed sides to the center of the square. Press one point onto the preserves. Brush a bit of egg wash on top of this point and press the other point on top of it. Be sure the Danish seals. You don't want it to pop open as it bakes.

20. Gently place the Danish on the prepared baking sheet. Repeat arranging, filling, and sealing the dough squares until you have six Danishes on each baking sheet.

21. Cover the Danishes with plastic wrap and allow them to rise for 30 minutes. As they are rising, preheat the oven to 400°F.

22. Before baking, brush the tops of the Danishes with the remaining egg wash. Bake for 18 to 20 minutes, until they are golden in color.

23. Remove the Danishes from the oven and place them on wire racks to cool. If using, make the glaze. Stir together the confectioners' sugar and 1 to 2 tablespoons of warm water. Drizzle the glaze over the top of each Danish.

Can't-Eat-Just-One Cinnamon-Cardamom Buns

MAKES 12 ROLLS

Almost every country has its own take on cinnamon rolls or buns. The inclusion of aromatic cardamom makes this Scandinavian version especially delectable. Serve with coffee or tea.

INGREDIENTS

FOR THE DOUGH

1 packet active dry yeast

¼ cup warm water

⅛ teaspoon salt

1 tablespoon granulated sugar

1 tablespoon unsalted butter, melted

6 tablespoons warm milk

1 large egg, whisked

½ teaspoon vanilla extract

1⅛ teaspoons ground cardamom

1¾ cups all-purpose flour

¼ cup unsalted butter, at room temperature

FOR THE FILLING

¼ cup granulated sugar

1 teaspoon ground cinnamon

Pinch of ground nutmeg

2 tablespoons unsalted butter, at room temperature

FOR THE ICING

½ cup confectioners' sugar, sifted

¼ teaspoon vanilla extract

2 teaspoons warm water

DIRECTIONS

1. For the dough, place the yeast and warm water in a small bowl and allow the yeast to dissolve. In a large bowl mix together the salt, sugar, melted butter, and milk. Pour in the yeast mixture, add the egg and vanilla and stir together until combined.

2. Whisk together the cardamom and flour.

3. Using either a wooden spoon or flat beater of a stand mixer, mix the flour into the warm milk mixture, beating until the dough is smooth and soft. Scrape down the sides of the bowl, form the dough into a ball, cover the bowl, and place the dough in a warm spot to rise for 1 hour.

4. Grease a large baking sheet. Lightly dust a clean work surface with flour.

5. Place the dough in the center of the work surface and sprinkle a little flour on the top. Using a rolling pin, roll out a large rectangle roughly 15 inches in length and 11 inches in width.

6. Spread half of the butter along half of the longer portion of the dough. Fold the unbuttered side over the buttered side and press together. Place the dough on the greased baking sheet, cover, and refrigerate for 1 hour.

7. Leaving the dough on the baking sheet, press it out into a rectangle roughly double in size. If using a baking sheet with raised edges or lips, press the dough to, but not over, the edges. You want the dough to remain on the bottom of the sheet. Spread the remaining dough butter over the center third of the

(Continued)

dough. Fold one unbuttered side to the middle and then fold the remaining unbuttered side over it. You are making three layers of dough that form a roughly shaped square. Cover and refrigerate again for 1 hour.

8. To make the filling, stir together the sugar, cinnamon, and nutmeg.

9. Dust the clean work surface with flour again. Grease a large baking dish and set aside.

10. Roll out the dough into a large rectangle roughly the same size as previously made. Evenly spread the butter over it and then sprinkle the cinnamon sugar over the top.

11. Using your hands, roll the dough into a cylinder. With a sharp knife cut it into 12 equally sized pieces. Each piece will be slightly wider than an inch.

12. Place the rolls, cut side up, in the baking dish, leaving about an inch of space between each. Cover them with a clean towel and allow them to rise for 45 to 60 minutes.

13. Preheat the oven to 375°F.

14. Bake the rolls for 15 to 20 minutes, until golden brown. Remove them from the oven, place the pan on a wire rack and cool slightly, about 15 minutes. Remove the buns from the pan to cool completely on the rack.

15. For the icing, whisk together the confectioners' sugar, vanilla, and water. Using a knife or spoon, spread or drizzle the icing over the rolls.

Persimmon Bread Bliss

MAKES ONE 9-INCH LOAF

Until my early 20s I knew nothing about persimmons. Then I moved to southeastern Pennsylvania, next to a family who possessed American and Hachiya persimmon trees and a desire to share their knowledge about homegrown foods. My first food lesson came one warm, fall afternoon as I bit into a horrible, mouth puckering, unripe persimmon. Turns out that persimmons taste best after the first frost. Exposed to the cold, the fruit's astringent flesh softens to a jam-like consistency and becomes juicy and honeyed in flavor. When ripe, persimmons are marvelous in a cobbler, crisp, pie, or quick bread. When unripe, they should be left alone. Trust me on that one.

Depending on the size of your persimmons, you will need to scoop out the flesh of as few as one or two persimmons to as many as four or five, to get 1 cup chopped persimmon for your puree.

INGREDIENTS

FOR THE PUREED PERSIMMON

1 cup peeled and chopped persimmon

1 teaspoon vanilla extract

2 tablespoons honey

FOR THE BREAD

2 cups all-purpose flour

2 teaspoons baking soda

Pinch of salt

1 teaspoon ground cinnamon

½ teaspoon ground nutmeg

1 cup firmly packed light brown sugar

2 large eggs, at room temperature

1 stick (8 tablespoons) unsalted butter, melted and cooled

¼ cup milk

¾ cup persimmon puree

1 cup diced pitted dates

½ cup golden raisins

DIRECTIONS

1. Preheat the oven to 350°F. Grease a 9-inch loaf pan and set aside.

2. To puree the persimmon, place the persimmon flesh, vanilla extract, and honey into the bowl of a blender and puree until smooth. Spoon out ¾ cup pureed persimmon and set aside.

3. For the bread, in a large bowl whisk together the flour, baking soda, salt, cinnamon, nutmeg, and brown sugar until well combined.

(Continued)

4. In a small bowl mix together the eggs, melted butter, and milk.

5. Make a well in the flour mixture and pour the liquids into the center. Using a spatula or wooden spoon, mix the dry and wet ingredients together. Add the pureed persimmon, dates, and raisins and stir until well combined.

6. Spread the batter in the greased pan and bake for 45 to 55 minutes, until a toothpick inserted in the center comes out clean. Cool 5 minutes before removing the bread from the pan and cooling completely on a wire rack.

How to Pick the Perfect Persimmon

Generally, markets carry two varieties of persimmons: the tomato-shaped Fuyu or the oblong Hachiya. Both come from Japan and possess a mild, honeyed, pumpkin flavor. Either will work in persimmon bread.

When picking persimmons, I look for unblemished, reddish-orange fruit that's so plump it looks as though it will burst through its skin. This is a ripe, flavorful persimmon. I avoid hard, yellow-to-pale orange fruit. These unripe persimmons possess an unpleasant, astringent taste that can only be remedied by freezing them.

If your only option is unripe persimmons, pop them into your freezer overnight. The next morning place them on your kitchen counter and allow them to thaw completely before baking or cooking with them.

Tropical Banana-Date Bread

MAKES 1 LOAF

Food-grade, unrefined, or "virgin" coconut oil provides both moisture and a tropical flavor to this classic quick bread. Unlike other oils, coconut oil has the consistency of softened butter and can replace butter, in a 1:1 ratio, in most recipes. Note that, because it comes from coconuts, the oil will contribute a coconut flavor to baked goods.

INGREDIENTS

1⅓ cups all-purpose flour

½ teaspoon baking soda

¼ teaspoon baking powder

¾ teaspoon salt

5 tablespoons coconut oil

⅔ cup granulated sugar

2 large eggs

1 teaspoon vanilla extract

3 very ripe or brown bananas, mashed

⅓ cup plus 1 tablespoon chopped dates

DIRECTIONS

1. Preheat the oven to 350°F. Grease a 9-inch loaf pan and set aside.

2. In a large bowl sift together the flour, baking soda, baking powder, and salt. Set aside.

3. With an electric mixer, beat the coconut oil and sugar until well combined, about 1 minute. Slowly add the dry ingredients, mixing until blended.

4. Whisk together the eggs and vanilla and pour them into the mixing bowl. Beat until incorporated.

5. Scrape down the sides of the bowl. Stir in the bananas and dates.

6. Spoon the batter into the prepared pan and bake until a toothpick inserted in the center of the loaf comes out clean, about 50 minutes. Remove the pan from the oven and place on a wire rack to cool for 15 minutes. Remove the bread from the pan, return the bread to the rack, and allow it to cool completely before cutting or storing.

Walnut Stollen Fit for a King

MAKES 2 LARGE LOAVES

Each year at Christmastime the German city of Dresden holds a holiday parade in which the star attraction is a loaf of bread. Far from just any old loaf, this 6,300-pound, sugar-blanketed, fruit- and nut-studded yeast bread, or stollen, journeys through Old Town Dresden on a horse-drawn cart. Accompanied by a procession of bakers and chefs who helped create this humungous baked good, the bread travels to the Striezelmarkt, or Christmas market. There it is sliced and sold to throngs of fans.

As someone whose childhood holiday meals often ended with a slice of soft, sweet, ground walnut-filled stollen, I was delighted to learn of this quirky custom. I was even more pleased to cover the Dresdner Stollenfest and sample several extraordinary versions of this sweet bread, including my beloved walnut stollen.

INGREDIENTS

FOR THE DOUGH

¼ teaspoon olive oil to grease the bowl

1 package dry active yeast

1 cup milk, at room temperature

1 teaspoon salt

4 cups all-purpose flour

10 tablespoons cold, unsalted butter, cut into chunks

4 large egg yolks, beaten

½ teaspoon vanilla extract

FOR THE FILLING

¼ cup unsalted butter, melted and cooled

1 cup firmly packed light brown sugar

2 large eggs, beaten

2 cups walnuts, ground in the bowl of a food processor or blender

1 teaspoon vanilla

⅛ teaspoon ground cinnamon

DIRECTIONS

1. Lightly grease a large bowl with the olive oil and set aside.

2. Place the yeast in a small bowl. Pour the milk over top of it and set it aside.

3. Whisk the salt and flour together in a large bowl. Add the chunks of butter. Using a pastry cutter or sturdy fork, cut the butter into the flour until incorporated.

4. Add the milk, eggs, and vanilla to the flour mixture. Using a spatula or your hands, mix together the ingredients until a soft dough forms, 5 to 7 minutes.

5. Shape the dough into a ball. Place it in the greased bowl and cover the bowl with a piece of plastic wrap. Put the bowl in a warm spot and allow the dough to rise for 1 hour or until it has doubled in size.

6. Once the dough has risen, make the walnut filling. In a medium bowl mix together the melted butter, brown sugar, eggs, walnuts, vanilla, and cinnamon. Set it aside.

7. Divide the dough into even halves. On a lightly floured work surface roll out the first half until you have a rectangle about 12 inches

wide and 18 inches long. Using a spatula or icing knife, spread half of the filling over the dough.

8. Repeatedly roll the dough over itself lengthwise—imagine this as rolling up a sheet of paper. Once you've finished rolling the dough into a log-like shape, cover it with plastic wrap and place it on a baking sheet. Put that baking sheet in a warm place.

9. Take the other dough half and repeat the above steps. Allow both breads to rise for 1 hour.

10. Preheat the oven to 350°F. Grease two baking sheets.

11. Place one loaf on each baking sheet. Bake the breads for 40 to 50 minutes, until golden brown on top. Remove the baking sheets from the oven. Allow the breads to cool for 5 minutes before removing them from the baking sheets and placing them on wire racks to cool completely.

Plush German "Plunder Squirrels"

MAKES 10 TO 12 ROLLS

In Germany this sweet roll is called a plunderhörnchen, which roughly translates to "plunder croissant," "plunder squirrel," or "Danish squirrel." It's an unusual name for an equally unusual treat, one that's shaped like a croissant, glazed like a doughnut, tender like a soft roll, and jam-filled.

In both Germany and Austria, plunder is a yeast-leavened dough used in sweet baked goods. Unlike croissant dough, plunder contains eggs. It also contains less fat than other pastry doughs. Similar to doughnuts and croissants, plunder squirrels taste best when eaten fresh. Enjoy your plunder squirrel on the go or with a cup of coffee, tea or milk.

INGREDIENTS

FOR THE DOUGH

1⅛ teaspoons dry active yeast

⅓ cup granulated sugar

¾ cup plus 3 tablespoons milk, warmed

1 large egg, at room temperature

3 tablespoons unsalted butter, melted

3 ¾ cups all-purpose flour

¼ teaspoon salt

FOR THE FILLING

⅓ cup mixed berry or other fruit jam

FOR THE GLAZE

1¼ cups confectioners' sugar, sifted

1 to 2 tablespoons water

DIRECTIONS

1. For the dough, place the yeast, sugar, and milk in a small bowl and allow the yeast and sugar to dissolve, 3 to 5 minutes. While you wait, whisk together the egg and melted butter.

2. Stir the flour and salt together in a large bowl. Make a well in the center of the flour and add the egg and milk mixtures. Stir the ingredients together until a rough dough has formed, about 3 minutes.

3. Place the dough on a flour-covered work surface and knead by hand for about 10 minutes or put the dough in the bowl of a stand mixer and, using a dough hook, knead the dough until a smooth, soft dough takes shape, 5 to 6 minutes.

4. Once the dough has reached the desired smooth consistency, place it in a bowl, cover it with a clean dish towel and allow it to rest and rise for 1 hour in a warm, draft-free spot.

5. Line two baking sheets with parchment paper.

6. After an hour, uncover and punch down the dough. Place it on a lightly floured work surface and, using a floured rolling pin, roll out the dough until you have a large rectangle roughly $1/8$-inch thick.

7. With a sharp knife cut the dough in half horizontally. Using your knife, cut 5 or 6 isosceles triangles (two sides the same size, one side a little longer) on the top half of the dough. Repeat with the bottom half.

8. If your triangles look too thick or small, run your rolling pin over them. Otherwise, center and place ½ to 1 teaspoon of jam toward the top of the triangle. Roll the long edge over on itself once and then over the blob of jam. Keep rolling until you reach the triangle's point. Tuck the point beneath the roll and place the pastry, point-side down, on the lined baking sheet. Repeat with the remaining cut dough.

9. Cover the baking sheets with plastic wrap and allow the plunder squirrels to rest for 20 minutes. Meanwhile, preheat the oven to 425°F.

10. Bake the plunder squirrels for 10 to 12 minutes, until the rolls are golden in color. Remove the pans from the oven and place the rolls on a wire rack. Cool completely before applying the glaze.

11. To glaze the pastries, mix together the confectioners' sugar and 1 tablespoon water; if the glaze seems too thick, add the remaining water. Brush the glaze over the top of each pastry and allow it to harden slightly.

Bewitching White Chocolate-Cranberry Panettone

MAKES 1 LOAF

With its lavish, cake-like dough and tall, mushroom-like shape, this Milanese bread is a stunner in both taste and looks. Traditionally, raisins, candied citron, and citrus zest fill out the bread, but in my version I use macerated dried cranberries and white chocolate chips. So decadent! So bewitching! So delicious that you'll want to bake this bread throughout the year!

INGREDIENTS

FOR THE STARTER

½ cup milk, warmed

1 package dry active yeast

1 cup all-purpose flour

1 teaspoon granulated sugar

FOR THE DOUGH

½ cup dried cranberries

¼ cup orange or cranberry juice

1 large egg

5 large egg yolks

1 teaspoon vanilla extract

⅓ cup granulated sugar

½ teaspoon salt

2 cups all-purpose flour, plus a little extra for dusting the work surface

3 tablespoons unsalted butter, softened and cut into chunks

¾ cup white chocolate chips

DIRECTIONS

1. For the starter, in a medium bowl add the milk to the yeast. Once the yeast has dissolved, about 10 minutes, add the flour and sugar and stir until well combined. Cover the starter with a sheet of plastic wrap and, placing in a warm spot, allow it to rise until double in size, about 2 hours.

2. For the dough, in a small bowl mix together the dried cranberries and orange juice. Set aside.

3. Grease a large mixing bowl and a panettone mold or 24-ounce coffee can. (If you do not have either a mold or empty coffee can, line a small, round, buttered baking dish or ovenproof bowl with buttered parchment paper—the paper should be roughly 6 inches high.)

4. Whisk together the egg, egg yolks, vanilla, sugar, and salt.

5. Add the starter and flour to the eggs and stir together. Once the ingredients are incorporated, place the dough on a floured work surface and knead for 5 minutes. Add the chunks of butter to the dough and knead it to incorporate. Continue kneading until the butter is completely mixed into the dough.

6. Form the dough into a ball.

7. Drain and pat dry the cranberries.

8. Flatten the dough, then add a third of the cranberries and white chocolate chips. Fold the dough over and knead in the cranberries and chips. Repeat until all the cranberries and chips have been added.

(Continued)

9. Form the dough into a ball. Place the ball in the greased bowl and cover it with plastic wrap. Put the bowl in a warm spot and allow the dough to rise for 1½ hours.

10. Once the dough has risen, punch it down and place it in the buttered panettone mold. Cover it with plastic wrap and give it one final rise, about 1 hour.

11. Preheat the oven to 350°F.

12. Remove the plastic wrap from the panettone and put the bread in the preheated oven.

13. Bake for 45 minutes or until a toothpick inserted in the center comes out clean. Cool completely on a wire rack before slicing and serving.

Acknowledgments

No one gets a cookbook, or any book, published completely on her own. I am no exception. I owe a huge thank you to Ariana Philips of JVNLA for her tireless advocating, enthusiasm, and support. I couldn't ask for a better agent. I likewise must thank Michael Tizzano, associate editor at The Countryman Press, for embracing the concept of moist cooking and this cookbook. Without you there would be no *Luscious, Tender, Juicy*. Thanks, too, to The Countryman Press associate art director Allison Chi for her guidance and patience.

I am indebted to my recipe testers, Vince Smith and Van Morgan, for ensuring that the directions made sense and the flavors paired well together. Thank you both! I should add that Vince was my chief recipe tester and retester, cheerfully tackling troublesome dishes and offering thoughtful suggestions.

Thanks to my taste testers, Sharon Burke, Kirsten Van Vlandren, Gwyneth Turner, Lenore Tichnell, Clint Tichnell, Laura Ransom, Tom Ransom, Michael Riley-Hill, Tony Riley-Hill, and Lindsay Herman. Whatever dishes I packaged up and dropped off at their front doors, they willingly tried and gave feedback.

Many thanks to Vasiliki Kolovos for sparking my interest in global cuisines, cooking, and baking. Her baklava recipe appears in *Luscious, Tender, Juicy*. Thanks to Jane and the late Frank Wilmer for teaching me about persimmons, elderflowers, morels, and countless other wild foods. I also must thank Luong and Mary Vo for sharing their knowledge of Southeast Asian cooking, Nancy Haberberger for Aunt Nancy's Stupendous Carrot Cake, and Elizabeth Theisen for her family piecrust recipe. Thanks, as well, to artist Gail Garcia and Elaine Arsenault for generously gifting Gail's hand-painted Dinner-Ware. Her ceramics appear throughout the cookbook.

I am grateful for my extraordinary "entourage," close, lifelong friends Marilee Morrow and Nickie Kolovos. They have joined me in countless culinary, and other, adventures, providing laughter and support in good and bad times. A nod, too, to friend and bon vivant Elliot Glickman, Susan Havison, Erin Hampton, and the Farmhouse Cooking students who encouraged me to write another cookbook.

Perpetual taste tester. Periodic sous chef. Intrepid traveler. Personal cheerleader. Sean Dippold does it all with good humor, wit, patience, and understanding. I am fortunate and grateful to have such an adventurous, fun loving, and encouraging spouse.

Bibliography

Alexander, Stephanie. *The Cook's Companion*. Camberwell: Lantern, 2004.

Alford, Jeffrey, and Naomi Duguid. *Hot Sour Salty Sweet*. New York: Artisan, 2000.

Beranbaum, Rose Levy. *The Baking Bible*. Boston: Houghton Mifflin Harcourt, 2014.

Boermans, Mary-Anne. *Great British Bakes*. London: Square Peg, 2013.

Child, Julia. *The French Chef Cookbook*. New York: Knopf, 2002.

Culinary Institute of America. *Baking and Pastry: Mastering the Art and Craft*. New York: John Wiley & Sons, 2004.

Culinary Institute of America. *The Professional Chef, 7th Edition*. New York: John Wiley & Sons, 2002.

Cunningham, Marion. *The Fannie Farmer Cookbook, 12th Edition*. New York: Bantam Books, 1993.

Daniel, Adrian, and Michael Daniel. *The Gate Vegetarian Cookbook*. London: Octopus Publishing, 2007.

Davidson, Alan. *The Oxford Companion to Food*. Oxford: Oxford University Press, 2006.

Edington, Sarah. *The National Trust Complete Traditional Recipe Book*. London: National Trust Books, 2010.

Egerton, John. *Southern Food*. Chapel Hill: University of North Carolina Press, 1993.

Green, Aliza. *Field Guide to Produce*. Philadelphia: Quirk Books, 2004.

Hahnemann, Trine. *Scandinavian Baking*. London: Quadrille Publishing, 2014.

Herbst, Sharon Tyler, and Ron Herbst. *The New Food Lover's Companion*. Hauppage, NY: Barrons, 2007.

Hesser, Amanda. *The Essential New York Times Cookbook*. New York: W. W. Norton, 2010.

Hoffman, Susanna. *The Olive and the Caper*. New York: Workman, 2004.

Hunt, Kathy. *Fish Market*. Philadelphia: Running Press, 2013.

Kenney, Matthew. *Matthew Kenney's Mediterranean Cooking*. San Francisco: Chronicle Books, 1997.

King Arthur Baking Company. *The King Arthur Flour Baker's Companion*. Woodstock, VT: The Countryman Press, 2003.

Librairie Larousse. *Larousse Gastronomique*. New York: Clarkson Potter, 2009.

Mason, Laura, and Catherine Brown. *The Taste of Britain*. London: HarperPress, 2006.

McGee, Harold. *On Food and Cooking*. New York: Scribner, 2004.

Nilsson, Magnus. *The Nordic Cookbook*. London: Phaidon Press, 2015.

Ojakangas, Beatrice. *The Great Scandinavian Baking Book*. Minneapolis: The University of Minnesota Press, 1988.

Page, Karen, and Andrew Dornenburg. *The Flavor Bible*. New York: Little, Brown and Company, 2008.

Rombauer, Irma S., et al. *Joy of Cooking*. New York: Scribner, 1997.

Scherber, Amy, and Toy Kim Dupree. *The Sweeter Side of Amy's Bread*. New York: John Wiley & Sons, Inc, 2008.

Slow Food Editore. *Osteria*. New York: Rizzoli, 2017.

Thom, Murray, and Tim Harper. *The Great New Zealand Cookbook*. Auckland: PQ Blackwell Limited, 2016.

Thompson, Alison. *Bake*. Camberwell: Penguin Group, 2011.

Weiss, Luisa. *Classic German Baking*. New York: Ten Speed Press, 2016.

Wolfert, Paula. *Couscous and Other Good Food from Morocco*. New York: Quill, 2001.

Websites and Articles

BERKELEY WELLNESS: "HOW MUCH
WATER IS IN YOUR FOOD?"
www.berkeleywellness.com/healthy-eating/food
/article/how-much-water-your-food

BUDAPEST COOKING CLASS: "HUNGARIAN
SOUR CHERRY PIE (MEGGYES PITE)"
budapestcookingclass.com/hungarian-sour-cherry
-pie-meggyes-pite-recipe

THE CAKE BLOG: "WHICH DAIRY
MAKES THE BEST CAKE?"
thecakeblog.com/2014/09/cake-baking-science
.html

HARVARD HEALTH PUBLISHING: "THE PROS
AND CONS OF ROOT VEGETABLES"
www.health.harvard.edu/staying-healthy/the-pros
-and-cons-of-root-vegetables

THE HONEY ASSOCIATION
www.honeyassociation.com

MENTAL FLOSS: "THE SCIENCE BEHIND
WHY PEOPLE HATE THE WORD MOIST"
www.mentalfloss.com/article/64984/science
-behind-why-people-hate-word-moist

MONTEREY BAY AQUARIUM SEAFOOD WATCH
www.seafoodwatch.org

SEMANTIC SCHOLAR: "AN EXPLORATORY
INVESTIGATION OF WORD AVERSION"
www.semanticscholar.org/paper/An-Exploratory
-Investigation-of-Word-Aversion-Thibodeau-Bromb
erg/47f8f255b95dcd55fbbf5cf0986ace8bc22575fd

SFGATE: "LIST OF FRUITS & VEGETABLE
WITH A HIGH WATER CONTENT"
healthyeating.sfgate.com/list-fruits-vegetable-high
-water-content-8958.html

Index